sean michael dever
Buddy Dog Art

1999 to 2015

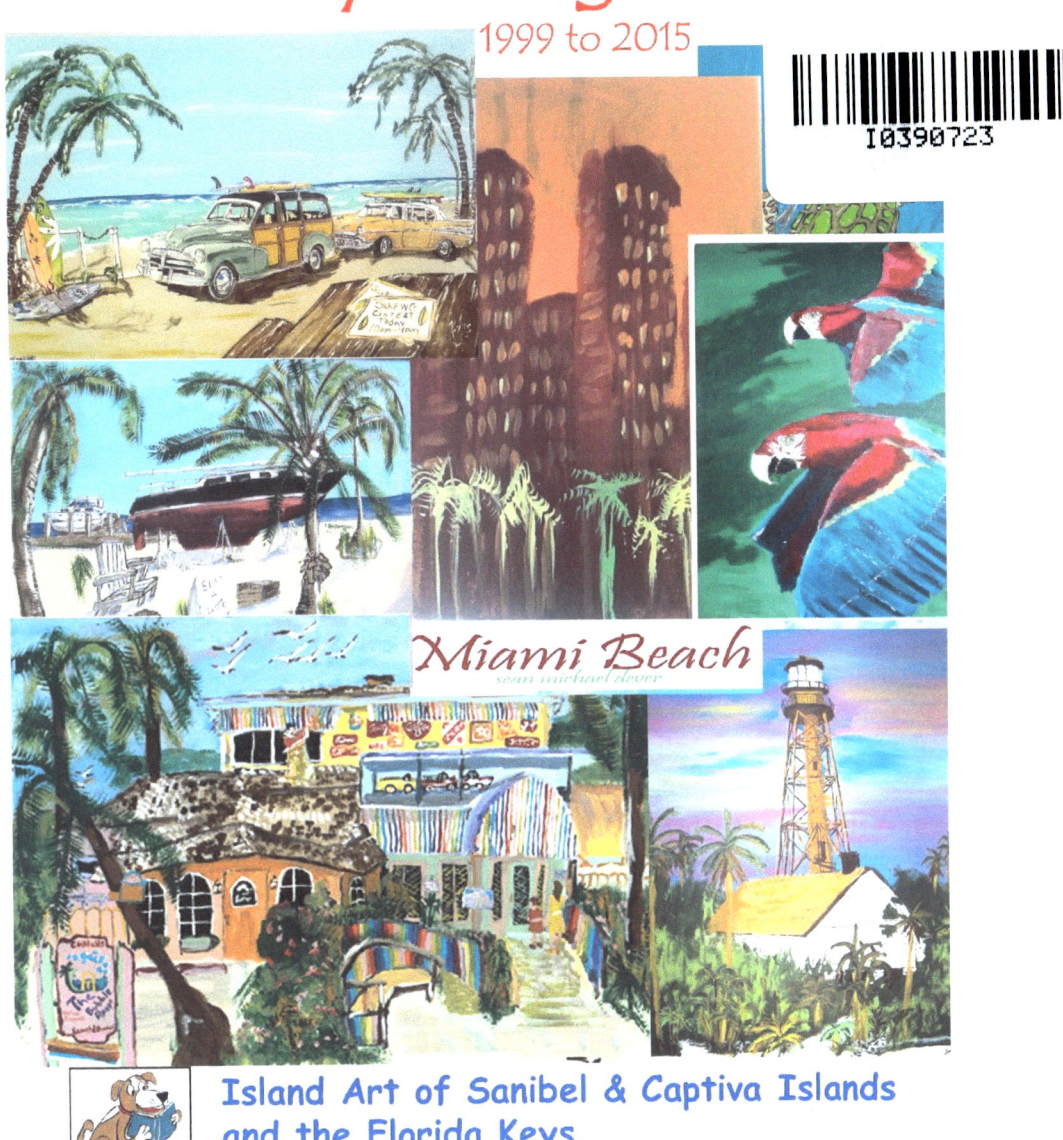

Miami Beach
sean michael dever

Buddydog Publishing & Enterprises

Island Art of Sanibel & Captiva Islands and the Florida Keys

Sean Michael Dever
Buddy Dog Art 1999-2015

Buddydog Book #300

By Sean Michael Dever
© Copyright 1998, 1999 - 2019

2019 Version Published by

Buddydog Publishing & Enterprises

Digital Kindle & Print Copies are distributed by
and may be ordered through
Amazon.com

ISBN 9781076225252

For more information on Sean Dever, his books, his contact information
Please go to his Author Page:

amazon.com/author/buddydog

Buddydog Publishing & Enterprises
Fort Myers, Florida

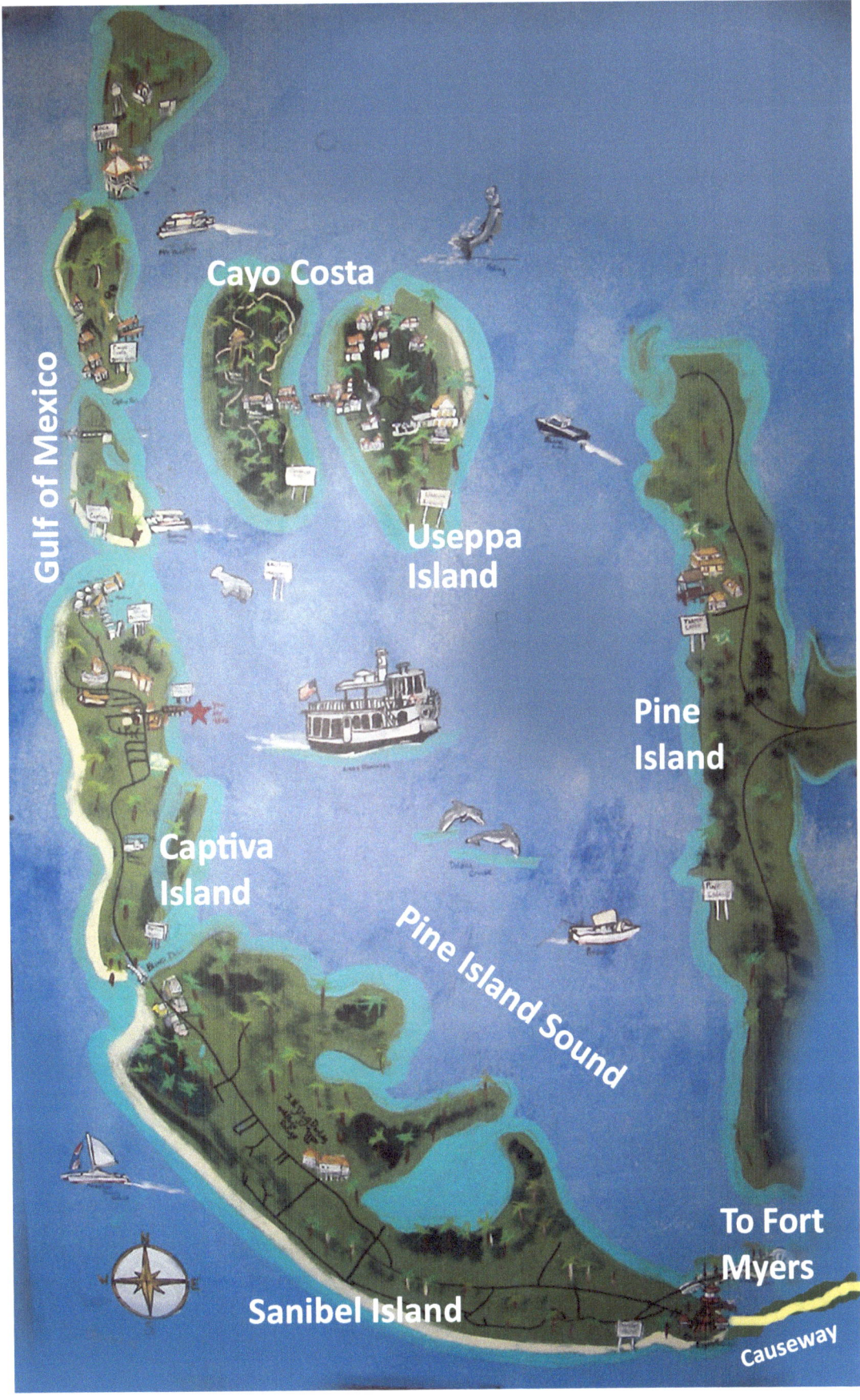

Cayo Costa

Gulf of Mexico

Useppa Island

Pine Island

Captiva Island

Pine Island Sound

To Fort Myers

Sanibel Island

Causeway

Other Books By Author Illustrator Sean Michael Dever

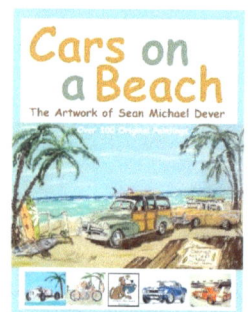 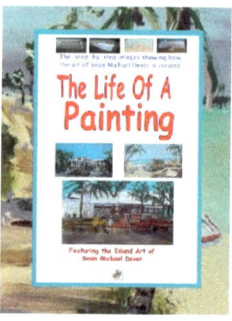 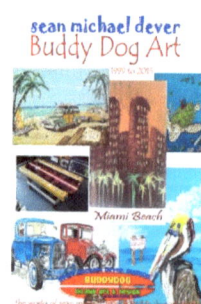 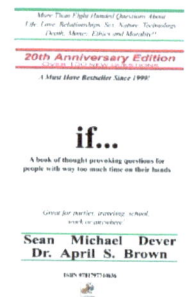

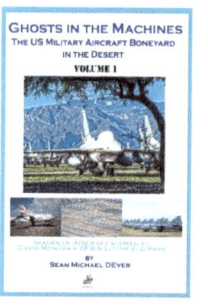 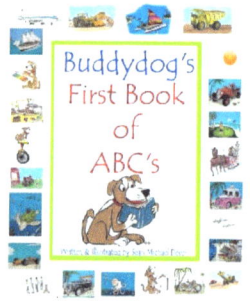 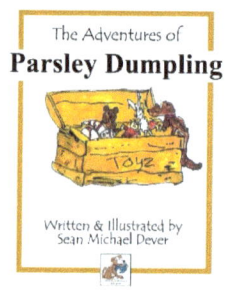 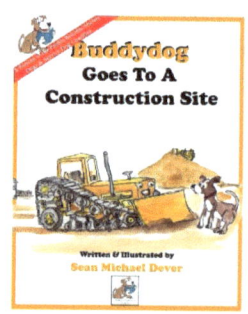

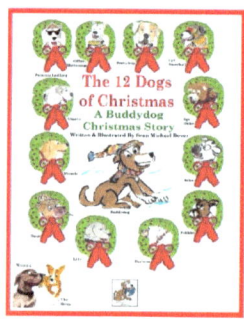 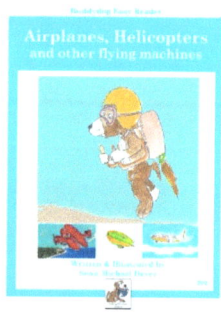 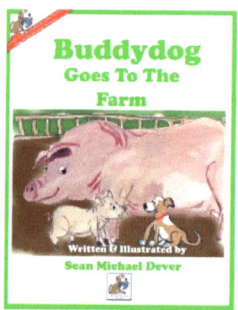 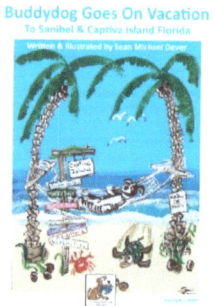

and many more!

To see more and/or order all of Sean Michael Dever's titles go to:
amazon.com/author/buddydog

About the Artist

"If, for just a moment, you get a longing for the shade of a palm tree, the feel of sand between your toes, a colorful rum drink with an umbrella, and the sound of steel drums, then I have done what I set out to do!" - Sean Michael Dever

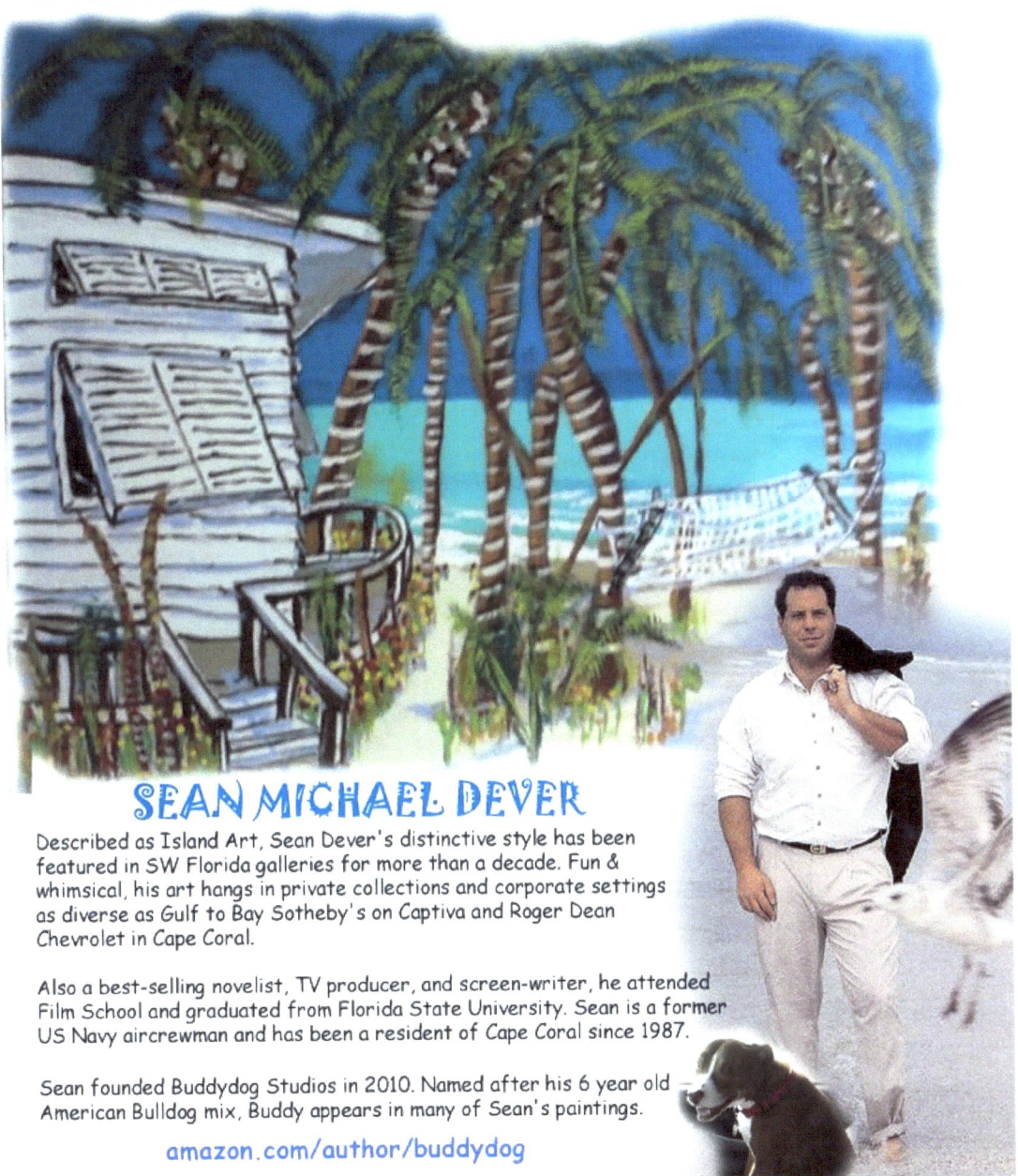

SEAN MICHAEL DEVER

Described as Island Art, Sean Dever's distinctive style has been featured in SW Florida galleries for more than a decade. Fun & whimsical, his art hangs in private collections and corporate settings as diverse as Gulf to Bay Sotheby's on Captiva and Roger Dean Chevrolet in Cape Coral.

Also a best-selling novelist, TV producer, and screen-writer, he attended Film School and graduated from Florida State University. Sean is a former US Navy aircrewman and has been a resident of Cape Coral since 1987.

Sean founded Buddydog Studios in 2010. Named after his 6 year old American Bulldog mix, Buddy appears in many of Sean's paintings.

amazon.com/author/buddydog

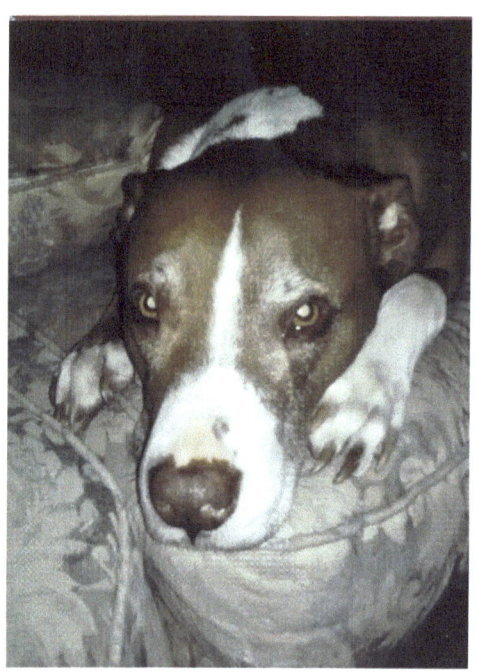

This book is dedicated to my family and
friends who over the years supported Buddydog
and me while we sold our art on Captiva.
I hope that all of you who have visited the islands
will enjoy the story and artwork of some of your
favorite places here on the islands. If you like
Buddydog, please order our other Buddydog
books on Amazon.com keyword: Sean Dever
Thanks!
-Sean & Buddydog

Most of the artwork inside was created between 1999 and 2015, although a few works were created back in the early 1990s and some as late as 2019. But the majority I created at my small Captiva Island, Florida studio where I would paint and Buddydog would greet everyone. This is not a complete collection of every painting I created. My automotive art is in another book, and my illustrations for my books are in those books.

-Sean Michael Dever

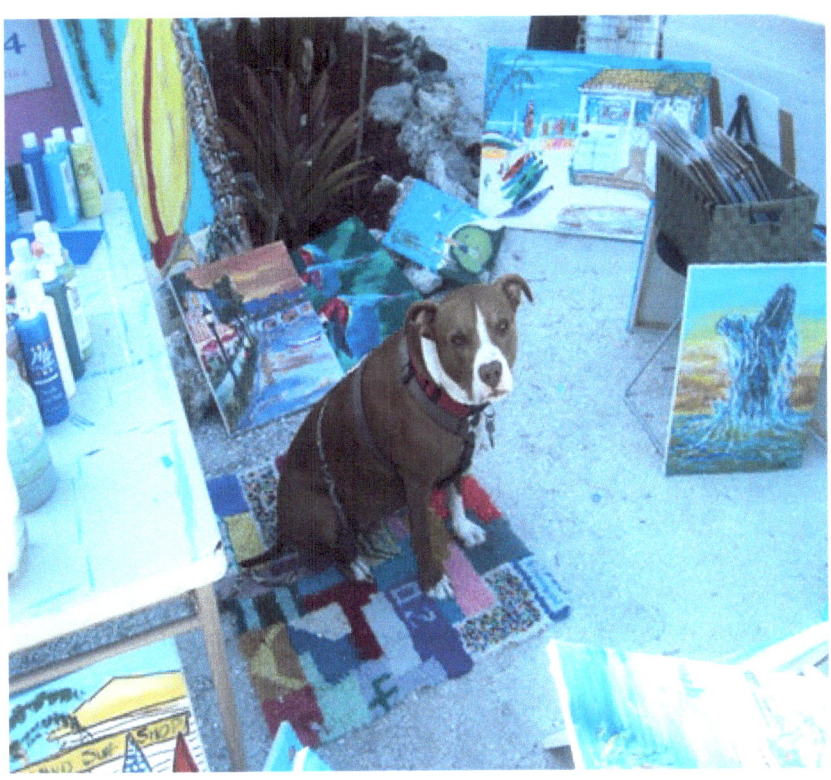

The Real Buddydog.

Table of Contents

Okay, so I kinda work on Island Time, so there is no table of contents. And the numbers next to the paintings aren't in order anyway. So, just look through the pretty pictures, drink something with some fruit and ice, and take a mental vacation, and come visit us when you can!

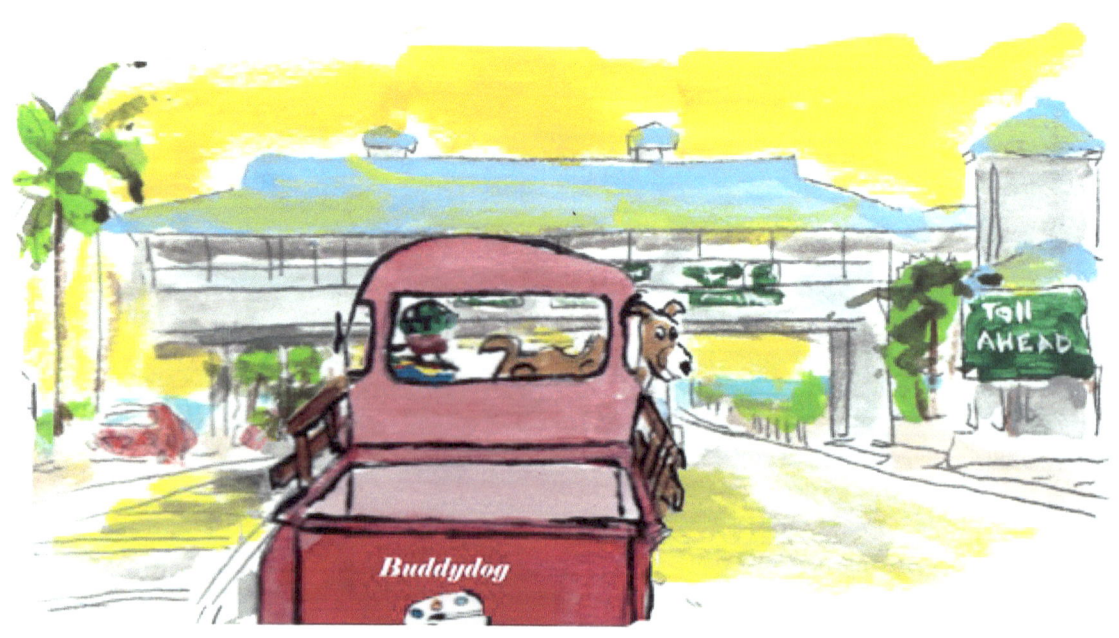

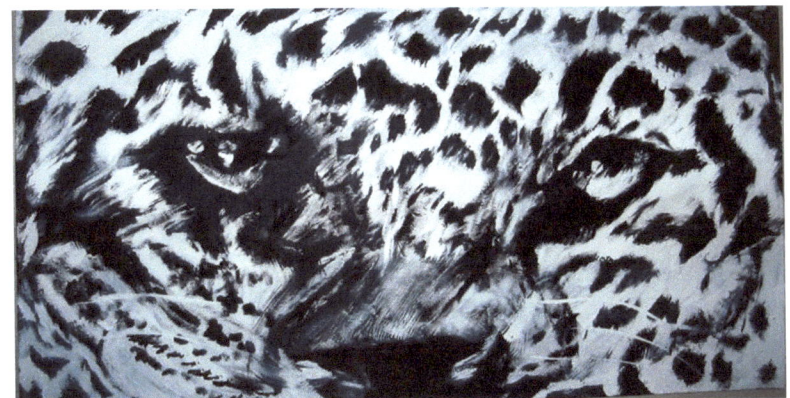

#058
snow leopard

#048 smiling pelican

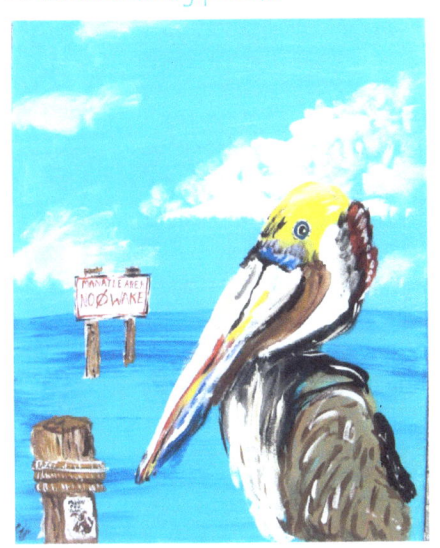

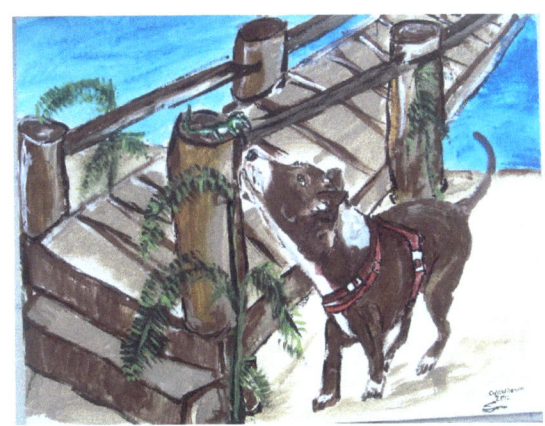

#045 Showdown

#050
flamingos
No.2

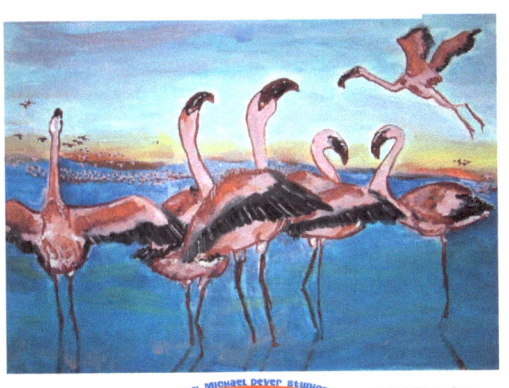

Pink Flamingos

 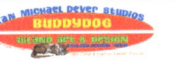 Limited Edition Print

#046

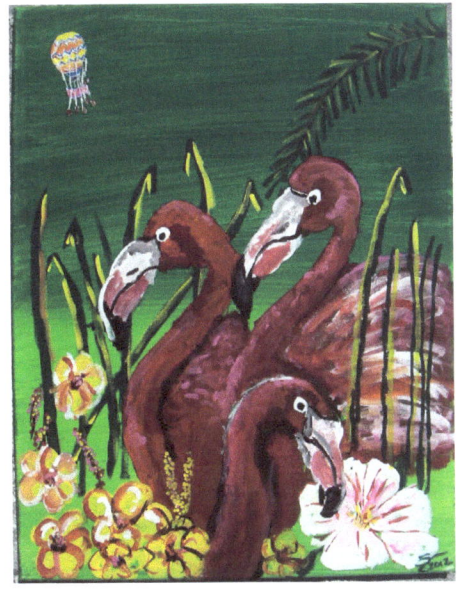

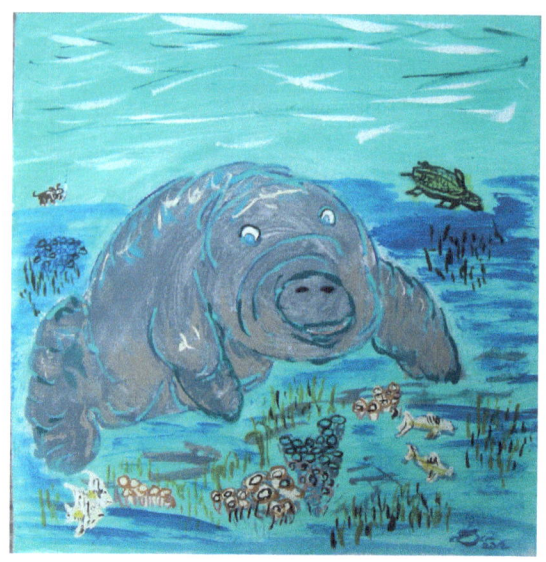

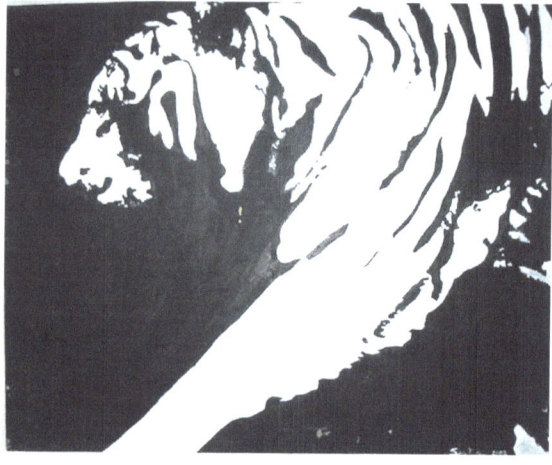

#062 tiger black & white

Manatee #2 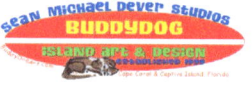 Limited Edition Print

#073

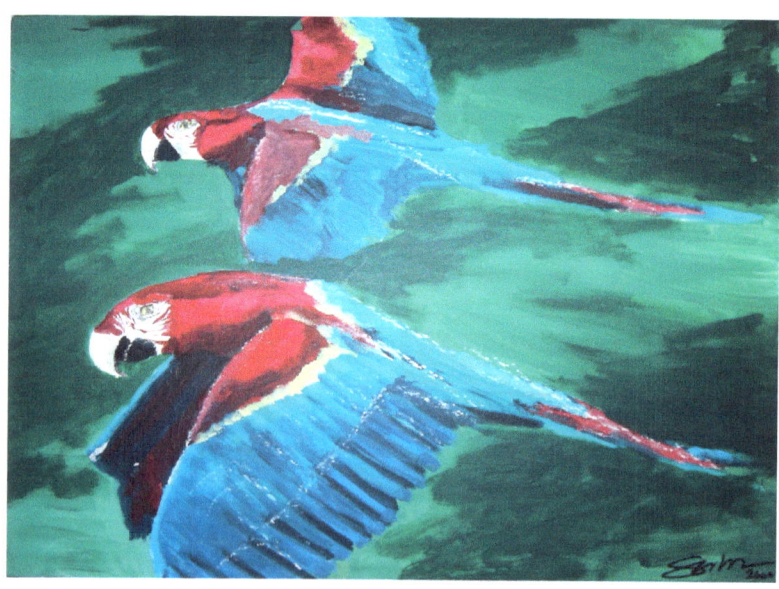

Wild Flight Limited Edition Print

#061

#005

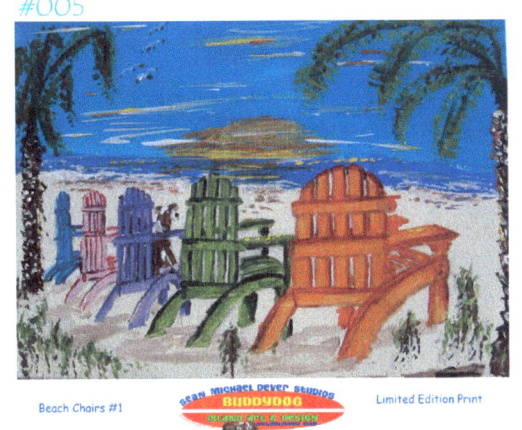

Beach Chairs #1   Limited Edition Print

#152

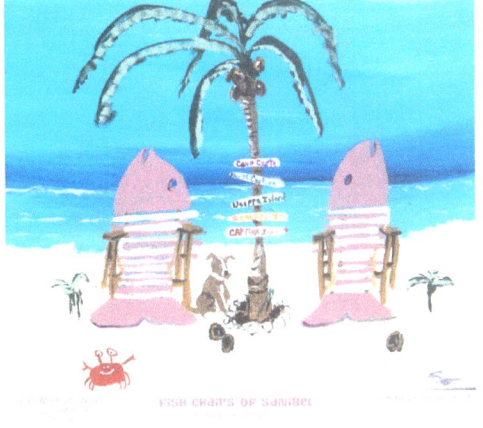

FISH CHAIRS OF SANIBEL

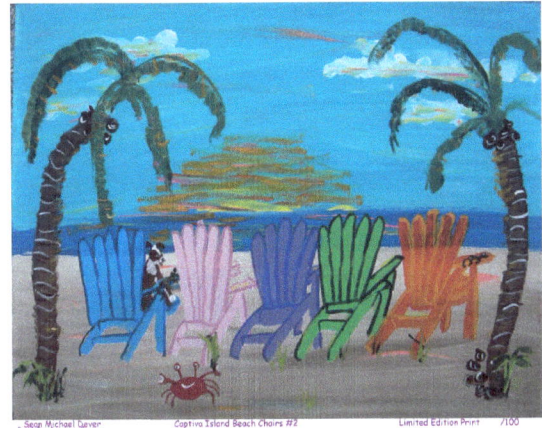

Sean Michael Dever
BuddyDogArt.com Captiva   Captiva Island Beach Chairs #2   Limited Edition Print   /100

#161

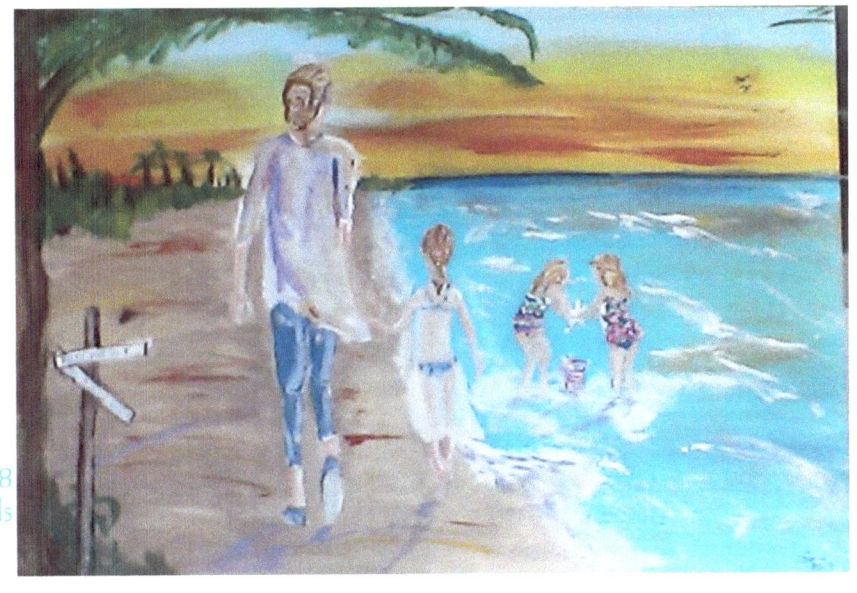

#488
gretchen & her girls

11

597 law office

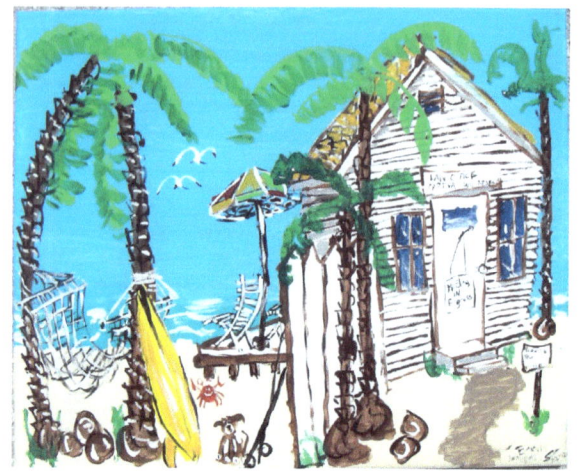

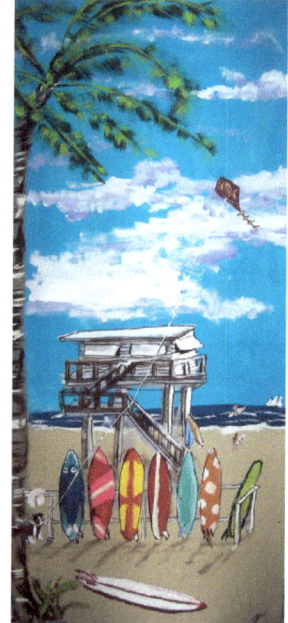

#003
Surfboards &
Kites

Acrylic On Canvas
2011

Sean Michael Dever
Limited Edition Print

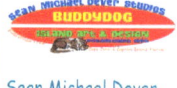

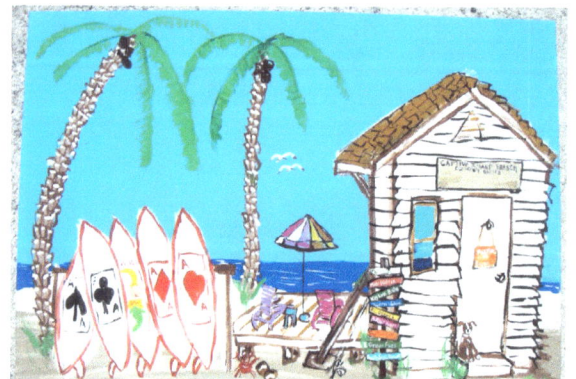

238 corporate office

601 beach branch office

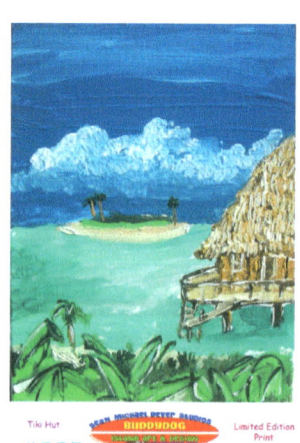

Tiki Hut   Limited Edition
                              Print
#025

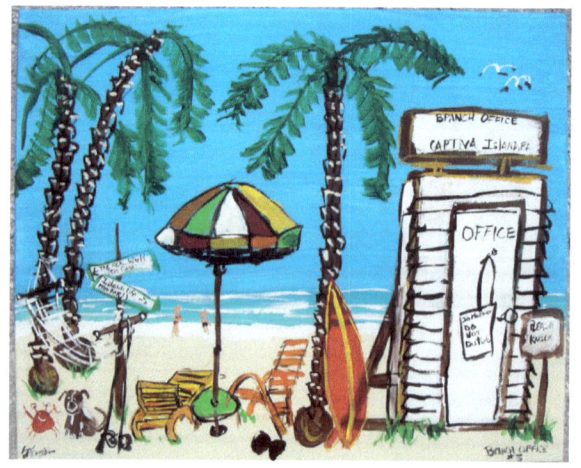

#1001 Miami Beach No.2

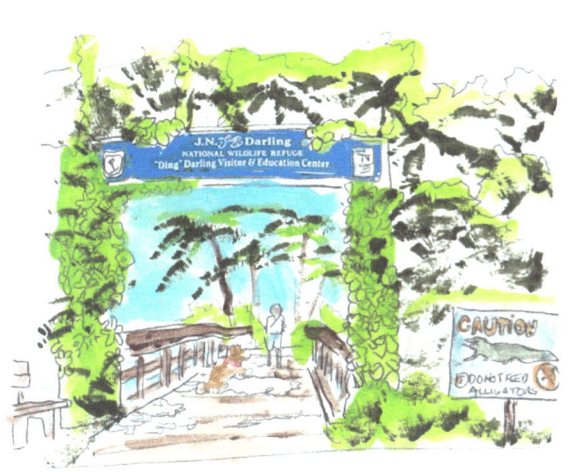

Ding Darling Refuge, Sanibel

miami beach

#597 bungalow No.2

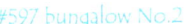

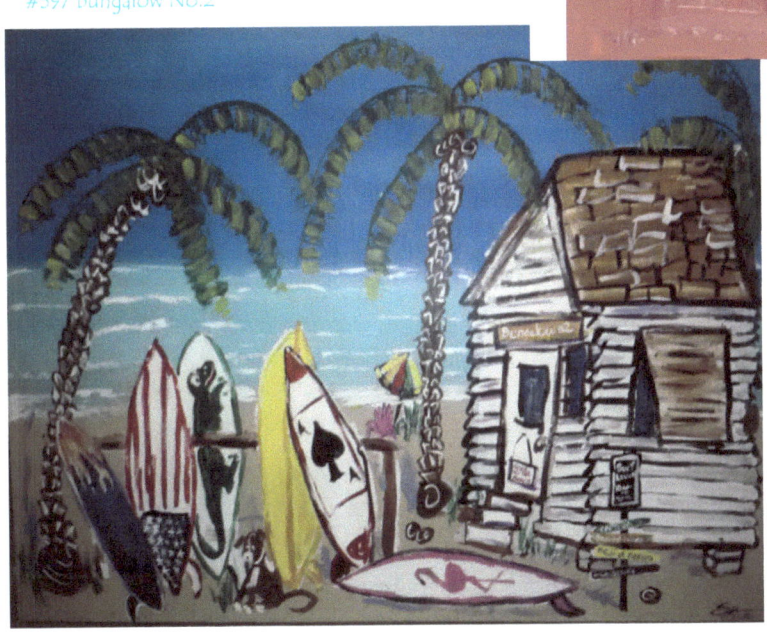

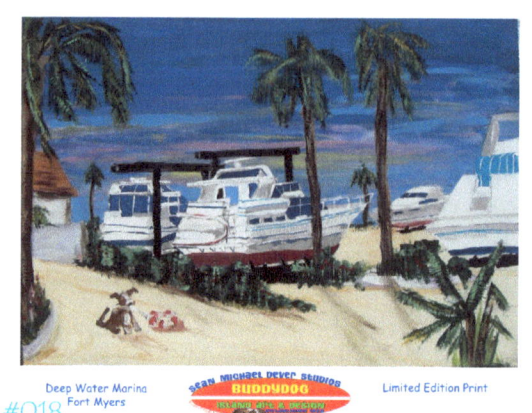

Deep Water Marina
Fort Myers
#018

SEAN MICHAEL DEVER STUDIOS
BUDDYDOG

Limited Edition Print

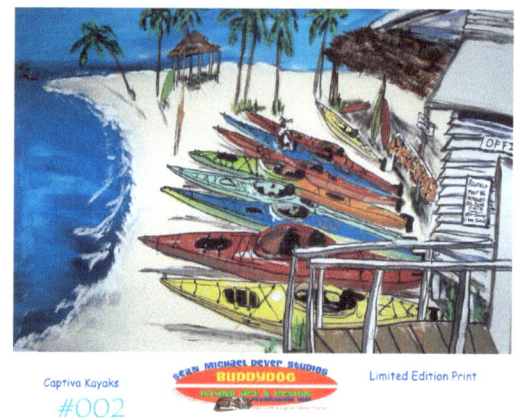

Captiva Kayaks
#002

SEAN MICHAEL DEVER STUDIOS
BUDDYDOG

Limited Edition Print

#069
cayo costa

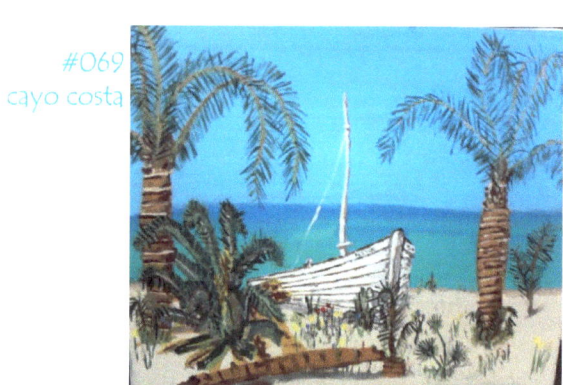

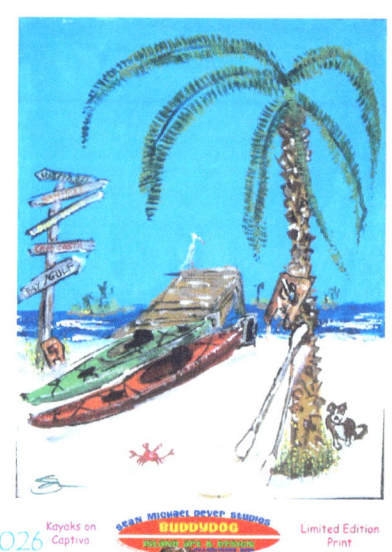

#026 Kayaks on Captiva

SEAN MICHAEL DEVER STUDIOS
BUDDYDOG

Limited Edition Print

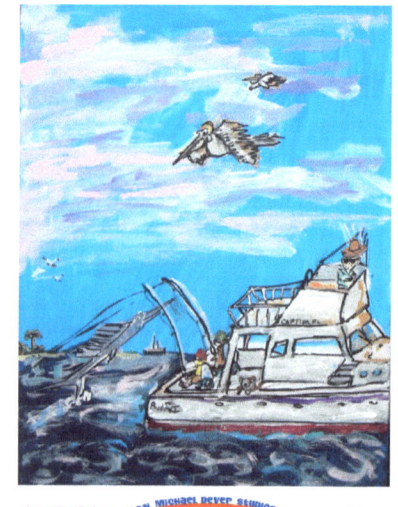

Deep Sea Fishing
Captiva
#024

SEAN MICHAEL DEVER STUDIOS
BUDDYDOG

Limited Edition Print

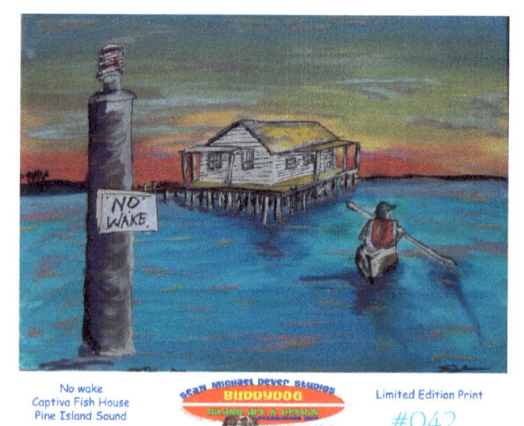

No wake
Captiva Fish House
Pine Island Sound
#042

SEAN MICHAEL DEVER STUDIOS
BUDDYDOG

Limited Edition Print

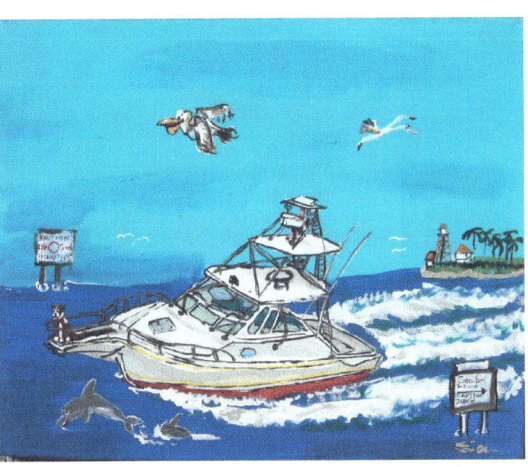

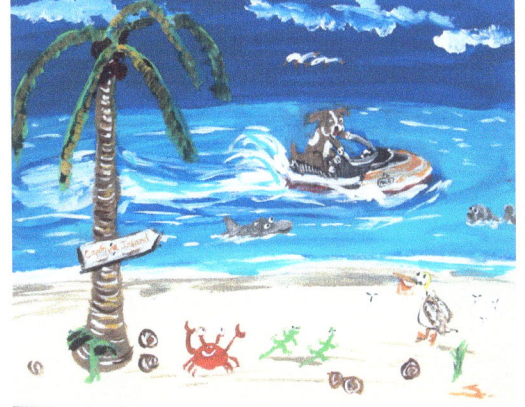

#172 buddy on a jet ski

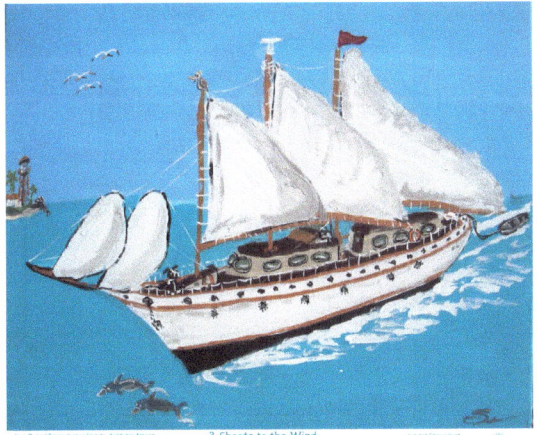

3 Sheets to the Wind

#142

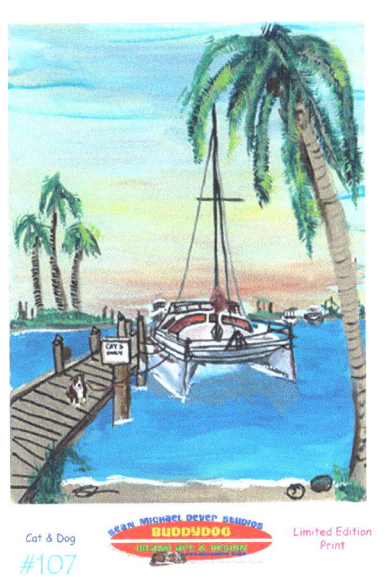

Cat & Dog

Limited Edition
Print

#107

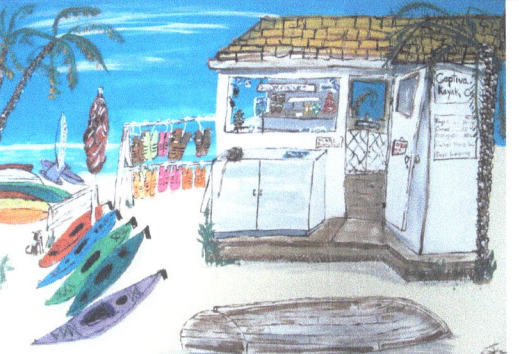

#120 Captiva Kyak Company

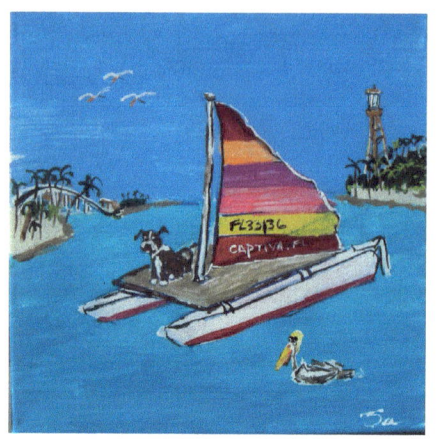

#129
Sanibel Island
Sail Cat & Dog

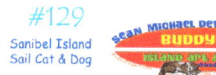
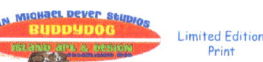

Limited Edition
Print

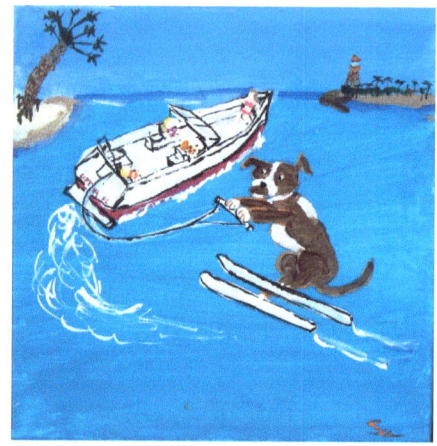

#098
Waterski
Sanibel Island

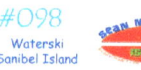
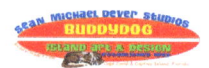

Limited Edition
Print

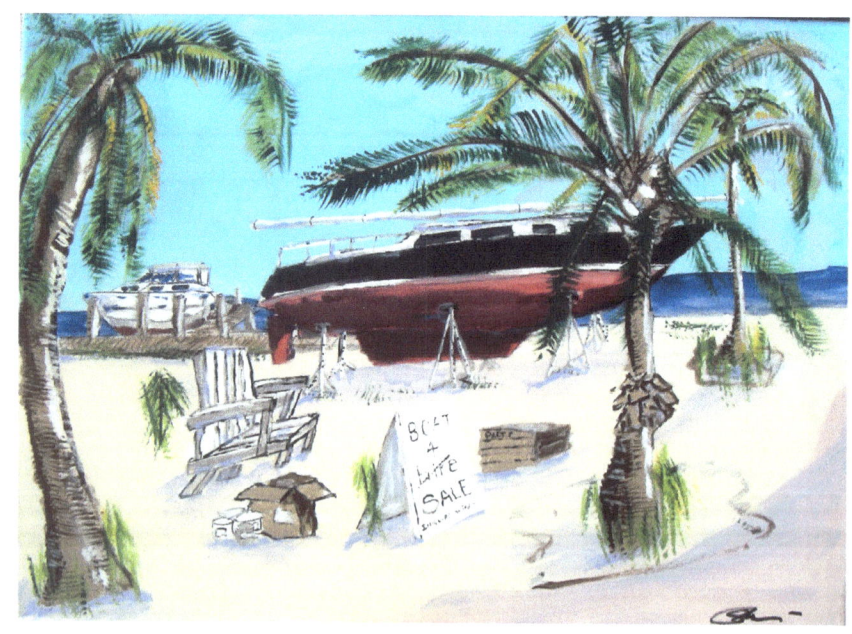

Boat 4 sale
#037

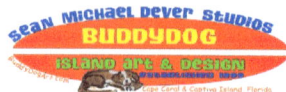

Limited Edition Print

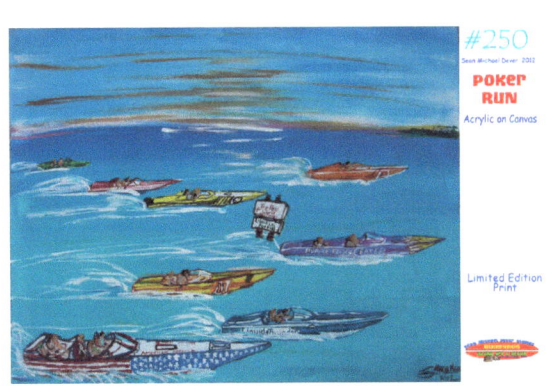

#250

Sean Michael Dever 2002

**POKER
RUN**

Acrylic on Canvas

Limited Edition
Print

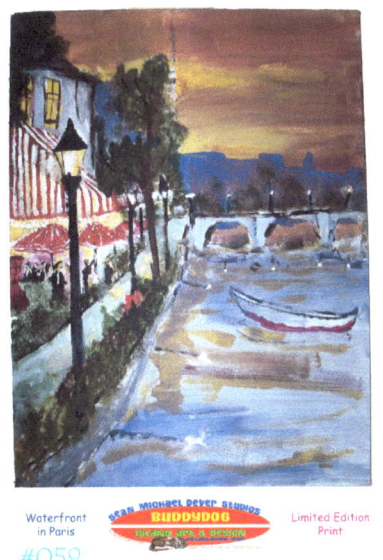

Waterfront
in Paris

#059

Limited Edition
Print

#267 gone fishin' no wke

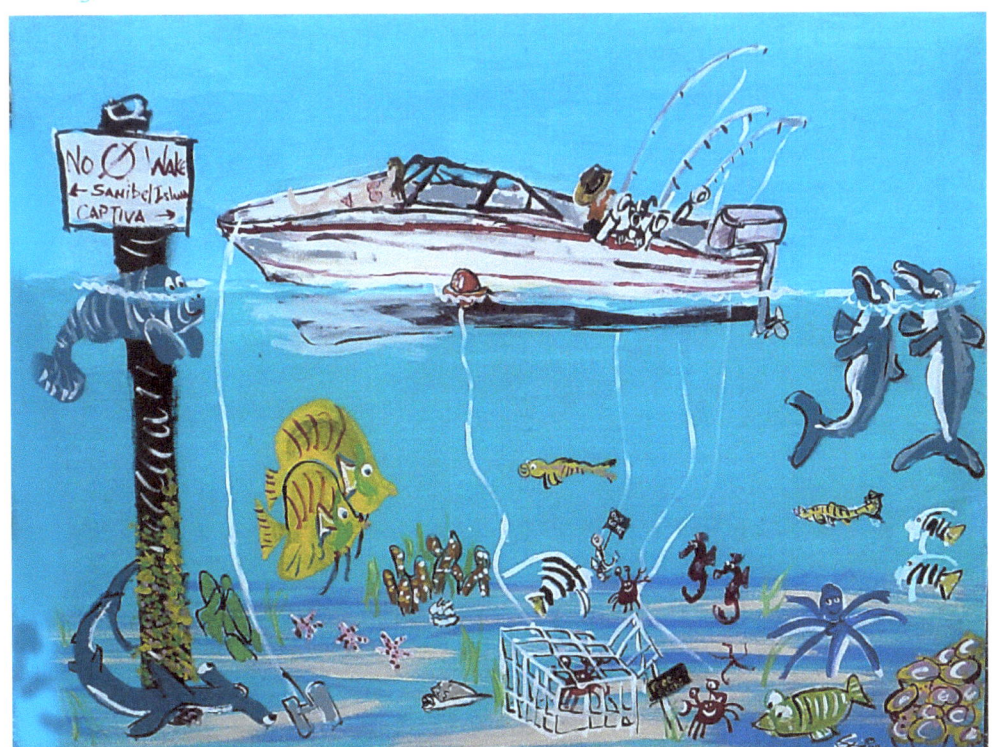

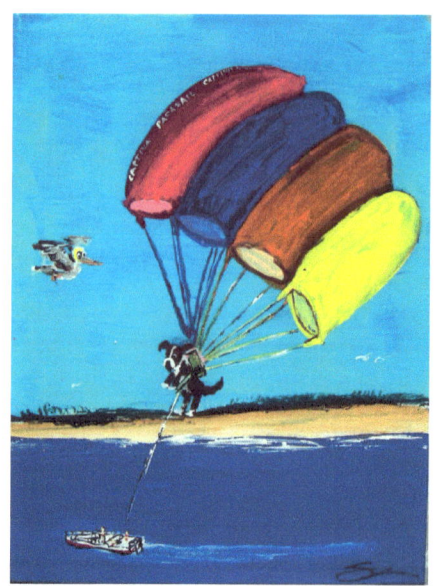

#039 captiva parasail
and pelican

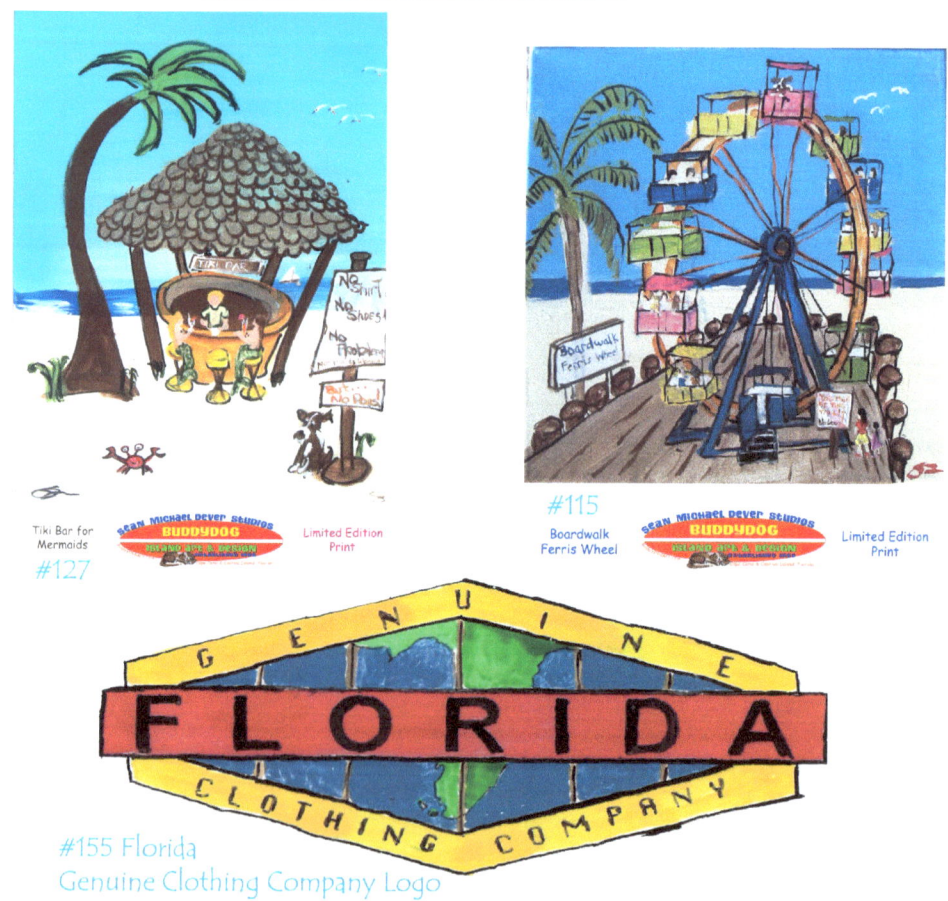

Tiki Bar for
Mermaids
#127

Limited Edition
Print

#115
Boardwalk
Ferris Wheel

Limited Edition
Print

#155 Florida
Genuine Clothing Company Logo

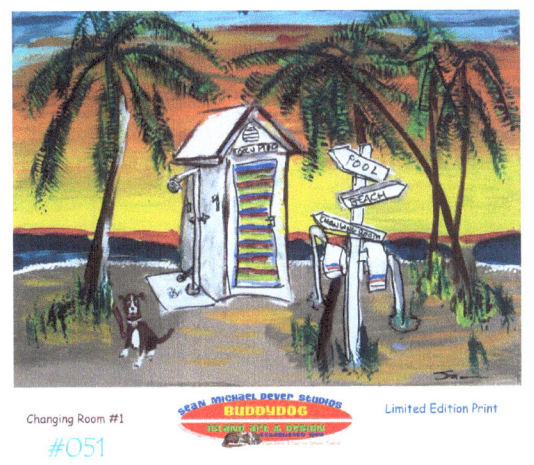

Changing Room #1   BUDDYDOG   Limited Edition Print

#051

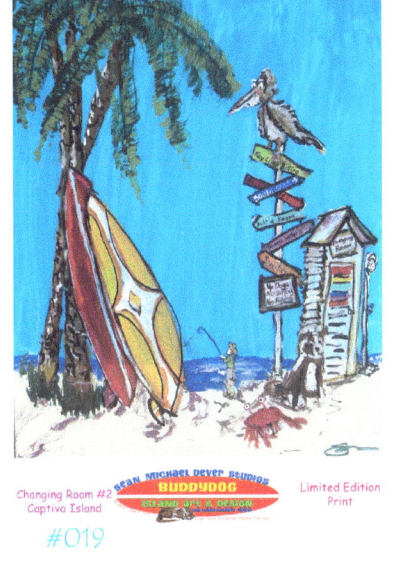

Changing Room #2   BUDDYDOG   Limited Edition
Captiva Island   Print

#019

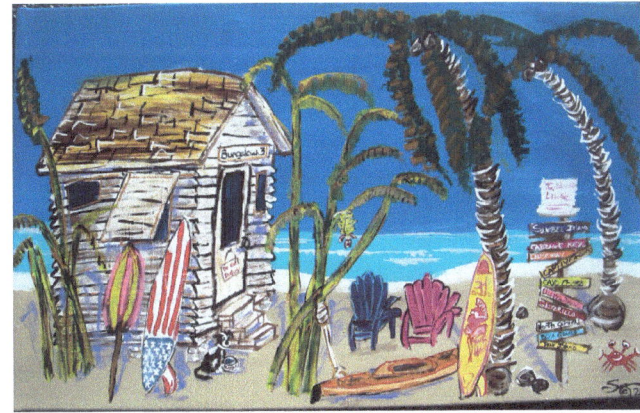

245 Bungalow #3

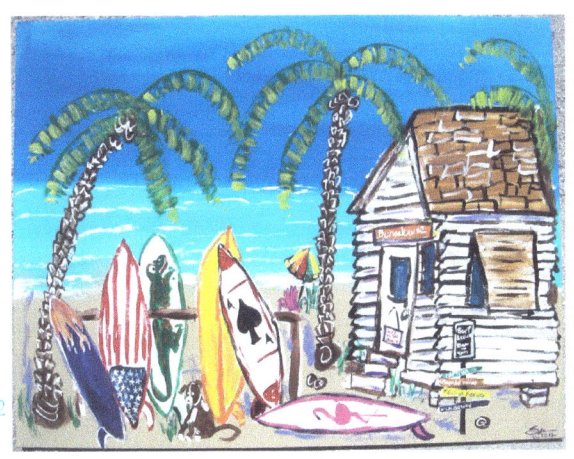

596
Bungalow #2

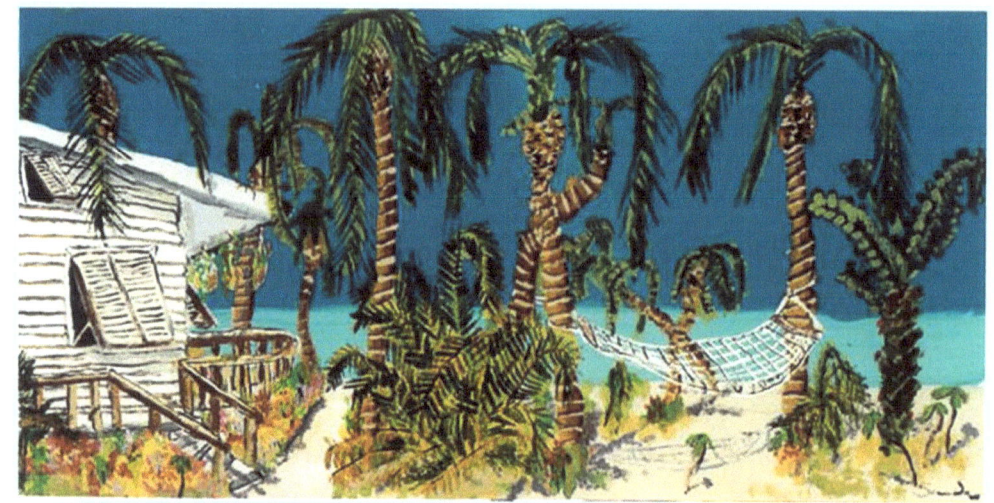

#006 captiva No.1

#081 Captiva No.3

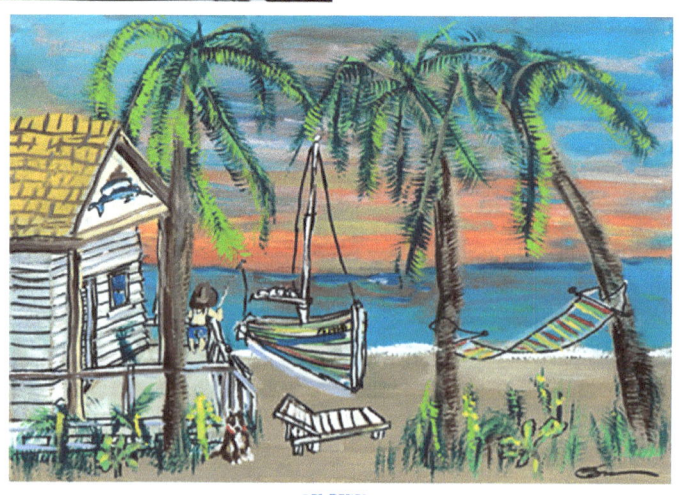

#021 Captiva #2

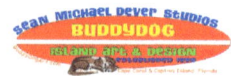

Limited Edition Print

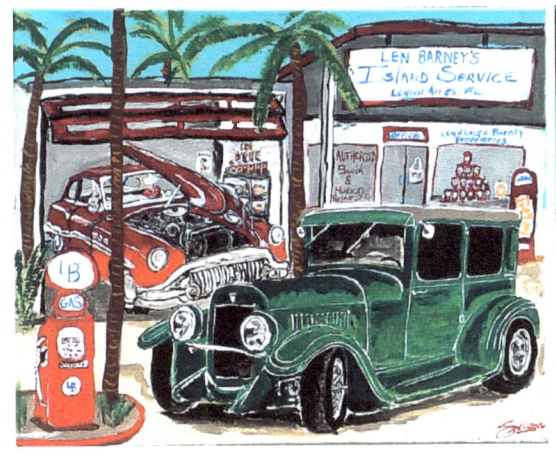

#623 Len Barney's 51 buick & 24 Hudson

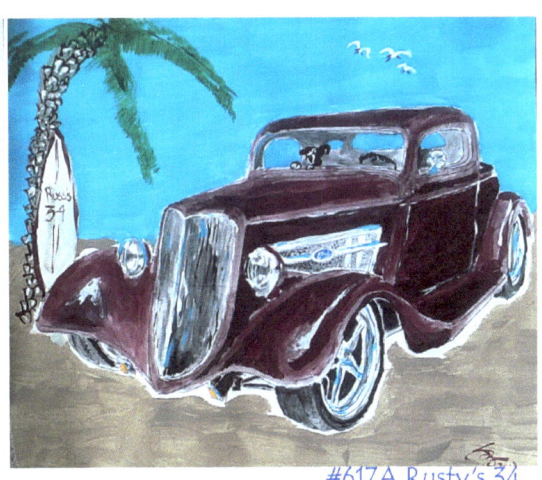

#624 Len Barney's 51 Buick & 24 Hudson

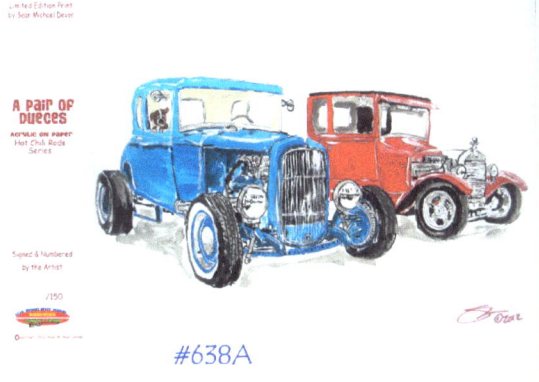

#638A

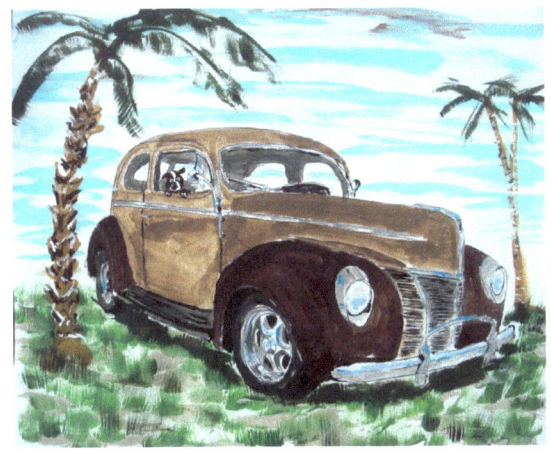

#617A Rusty's 34

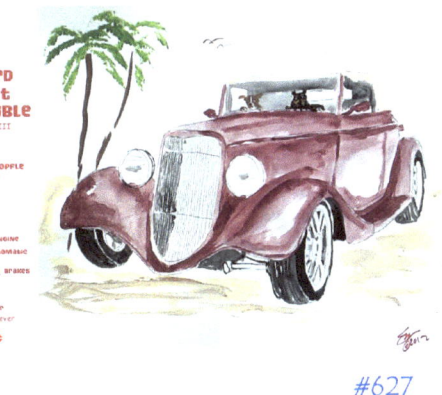

#650 1940 Ford

#627

21

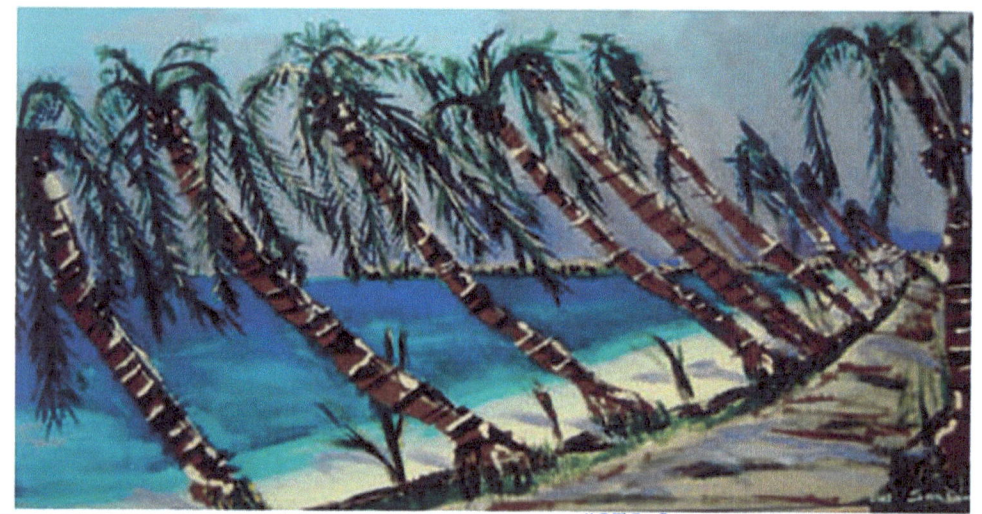

#070 Causeway No.2

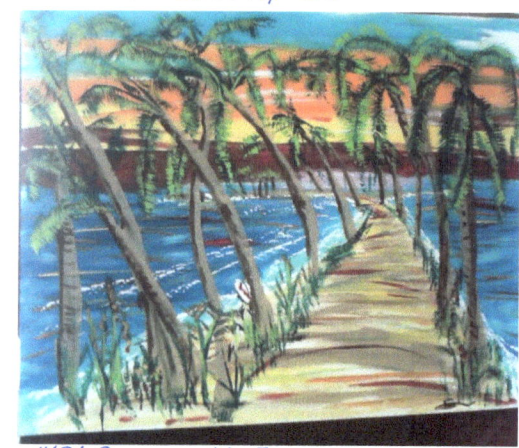

#243 Island Time

#126 Causeway No.3

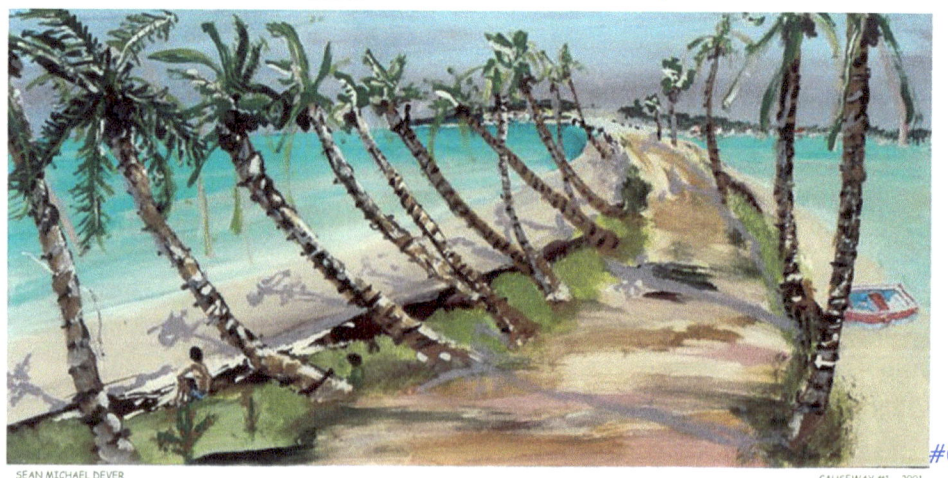

#035

SEAN MICHAEL DEVER

CAUSEWAY #1   2001

22

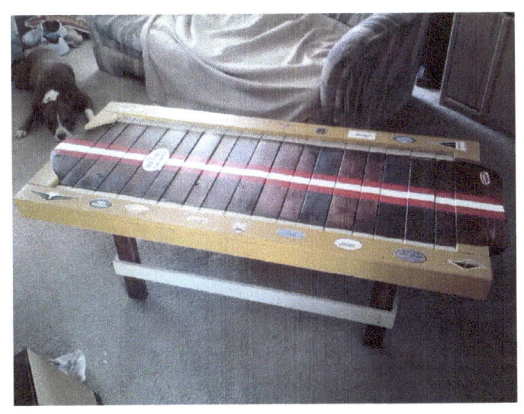

Classic

Surfboard

Table

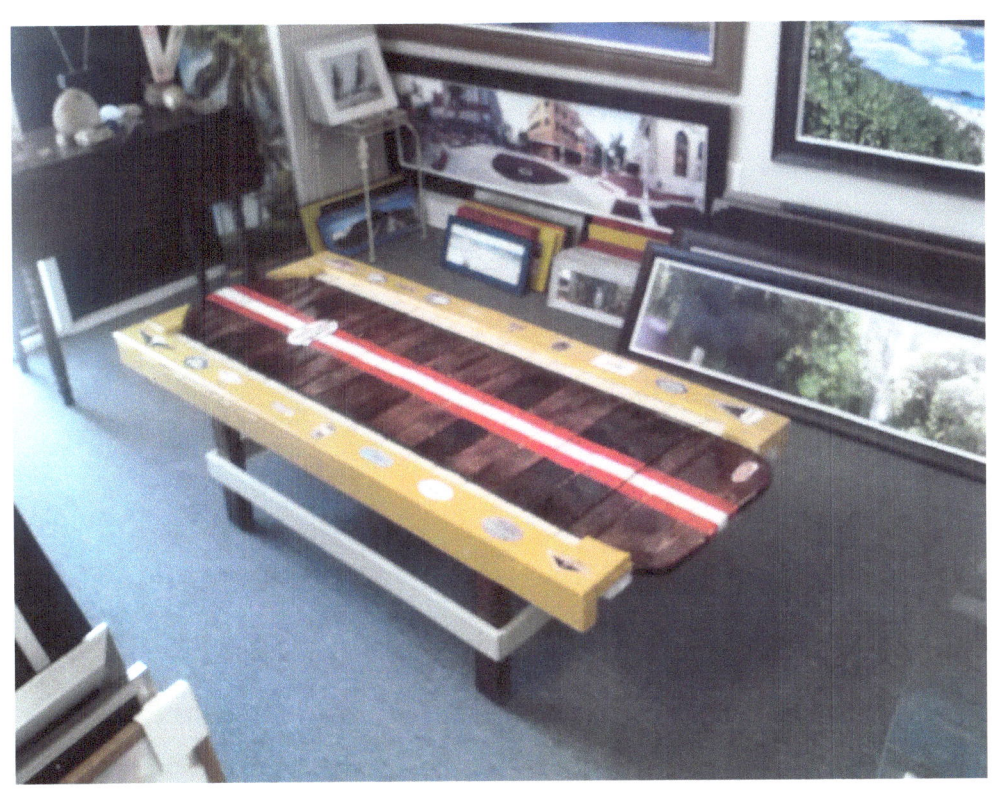

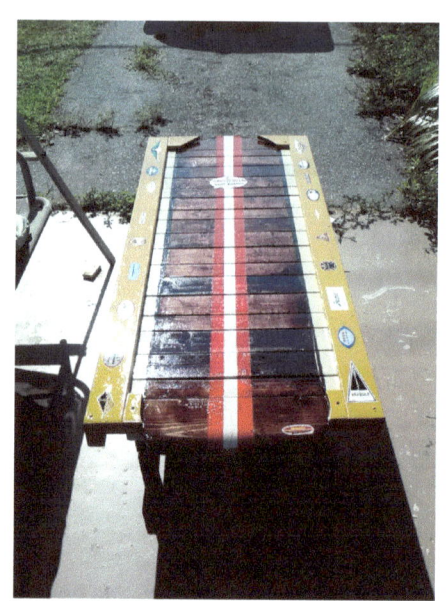

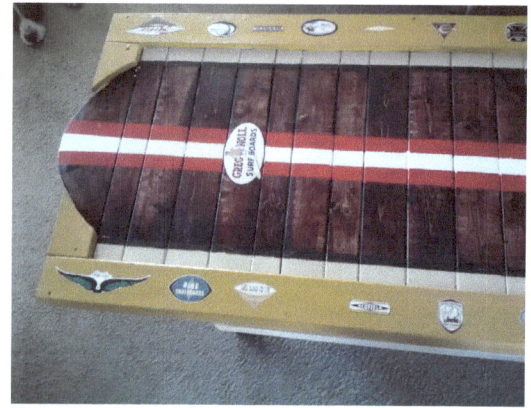

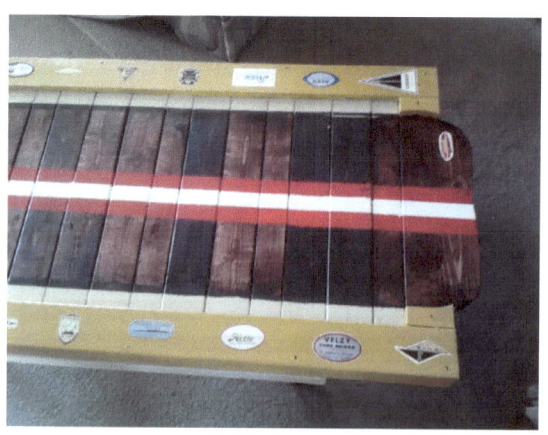

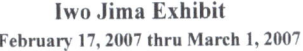

Iwo Jima Exhibit
February 17, 2007 thru March 1, 2007

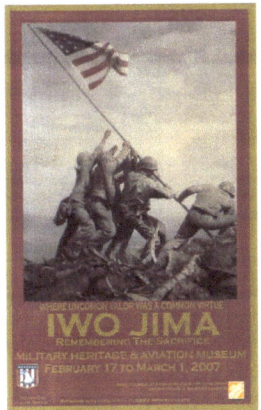

11x17 Limited Edition Numbered Prints
suitable for framing available for a donation of $19.45

This display made possible by a donation from Home Depot of Punta Gorda,
Tim Dever, & Majestic Cabinets

#145 Iwo Jima Exhibit Poster 2007

PIRATE FLAGS IN HISTORY

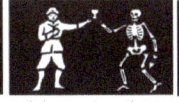

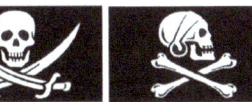

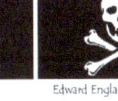

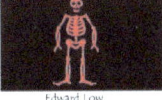

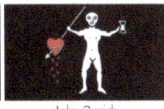

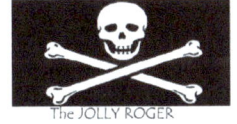
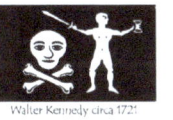

CAPTIVA ISLAND
FLORIDA

#106 Pirate Flags in History

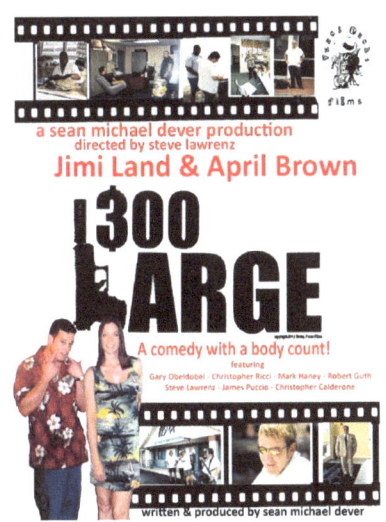

#1106 young punks films 300 large dvd cover
2003/2014

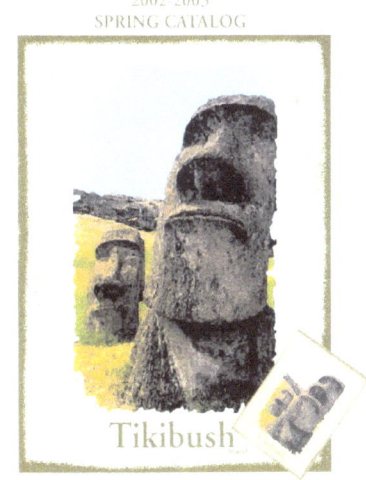

#156 Tikibush Clothing Company Logo
1999

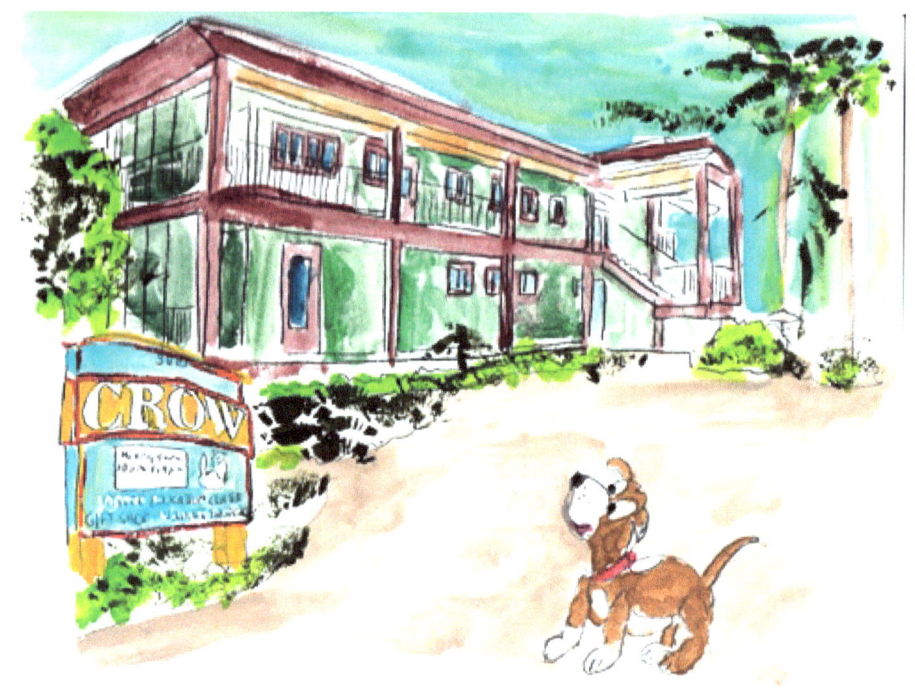

CROW Wildlife Rehab, Sanibel Island

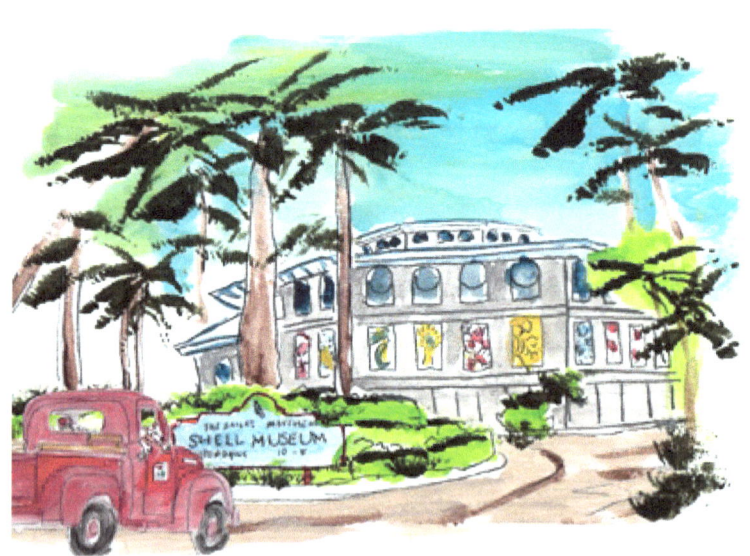

Bailey Shell Museum, Sanibel Island

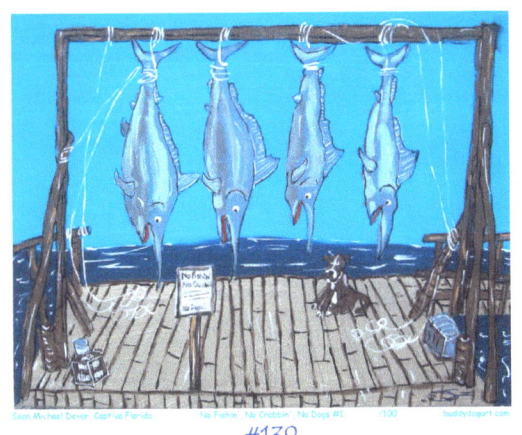

#139

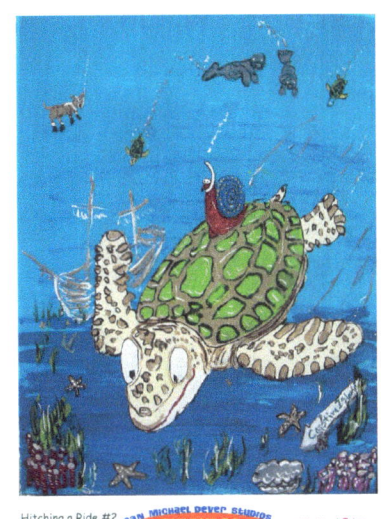

Hitching a Ride #2
Sea Turtle

Limited Edition
Print

#131

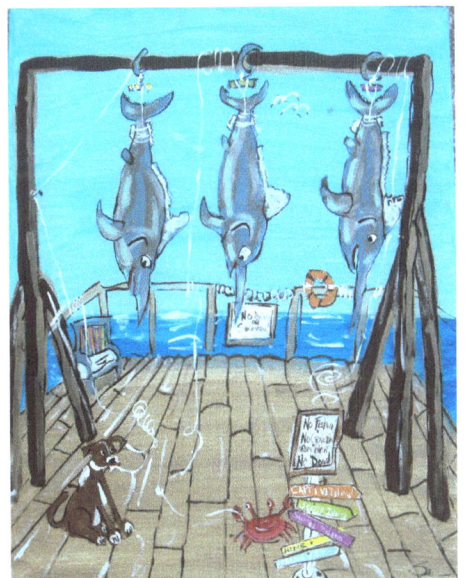
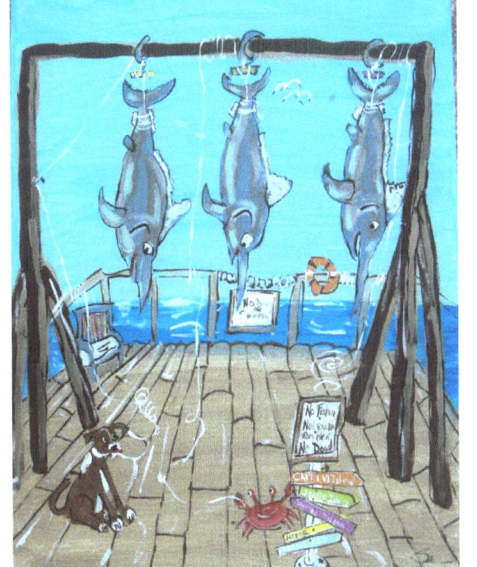
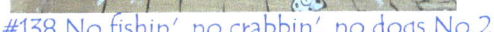

#138 No fishin', no crabbin', no dogs No.2

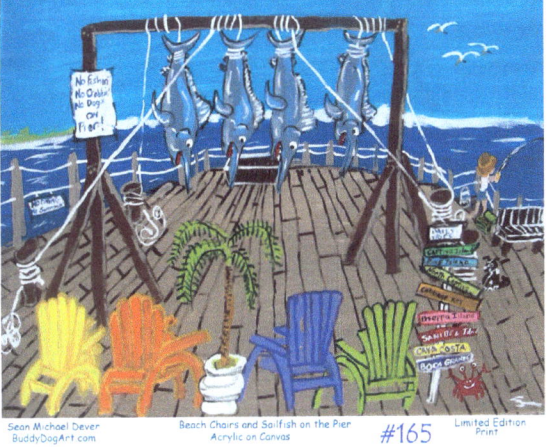

Sean Michael Dever
BuddyDogArt.com

Beach Chairs and Sailfish on the Pier
Acrylic on Canvas

#165

Limited Edition
Print

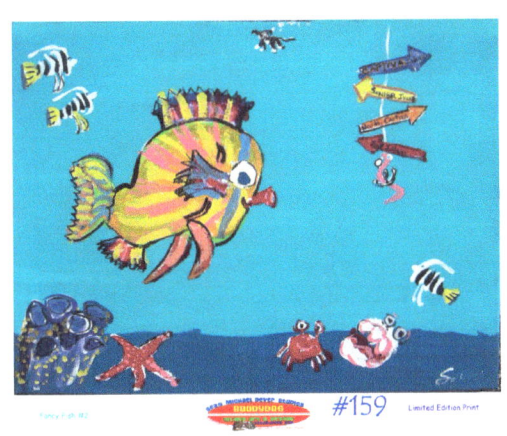

#159   Limited Edition Print

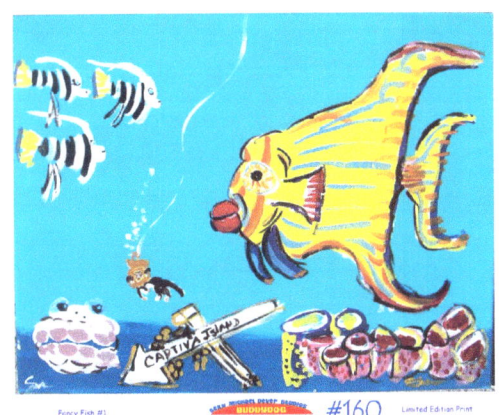

Fancy Fish #1   #160   Limited Edition Print

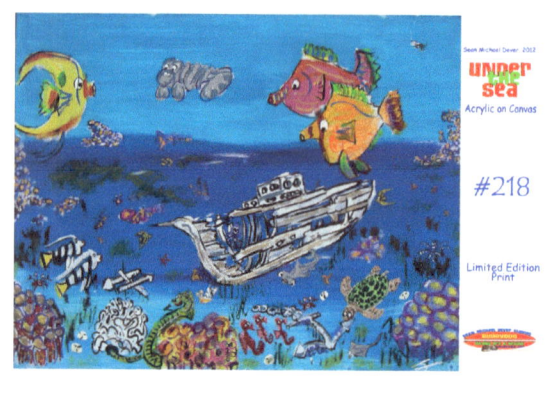

Sean Michael Dever 2012

UNDER THE SEA

Acrylic on Canvas

#218

Limited Edition Print

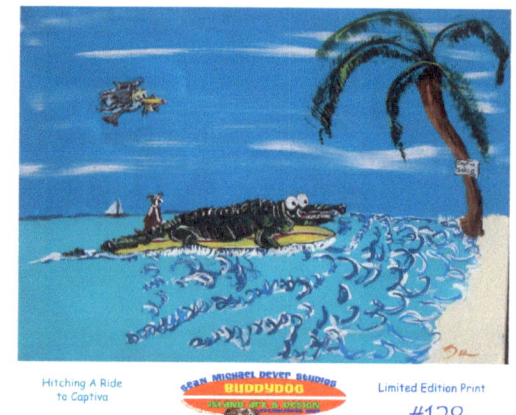

Hitching A Ride
to Captiva

BUDDYDOG

Limited Edition Print

#128

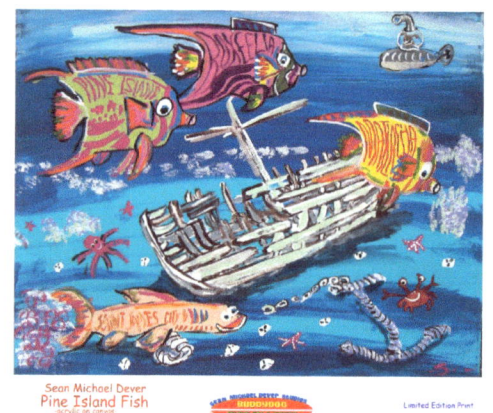

Sean Michael Dever
Pine Island Fish
acrylic on canvas

BUDDYDOG

Limited Edition Print

#201

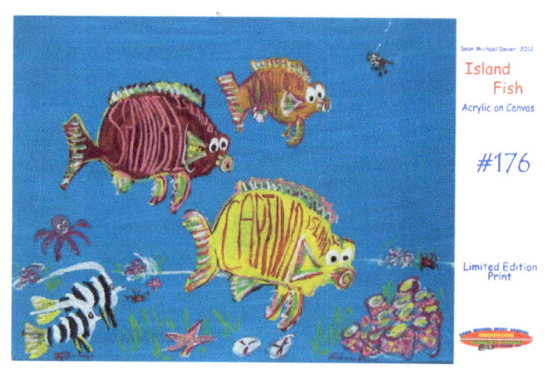

Sean Michael Dever 2012

Island Fish

Acrylic on Canvas

#176

Limited Edition Print

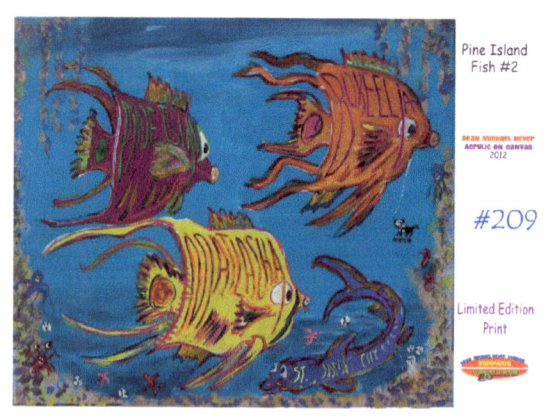

Pine Island
Fish #2

SEAN MICHAEL DEVER
ACRYLIC ON CANVAS
2012

#209

Limited Edition
Print

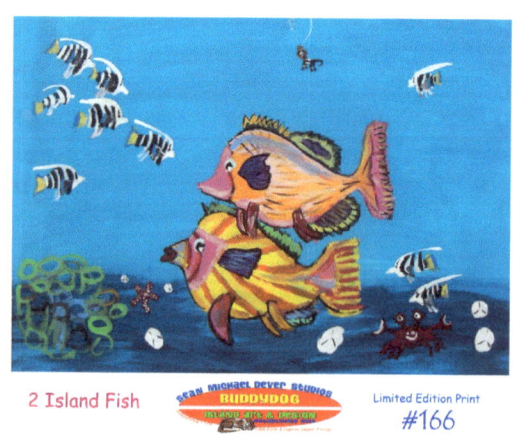

2 Island Fish

BUDDYDOG

Limited Edition Print

#166

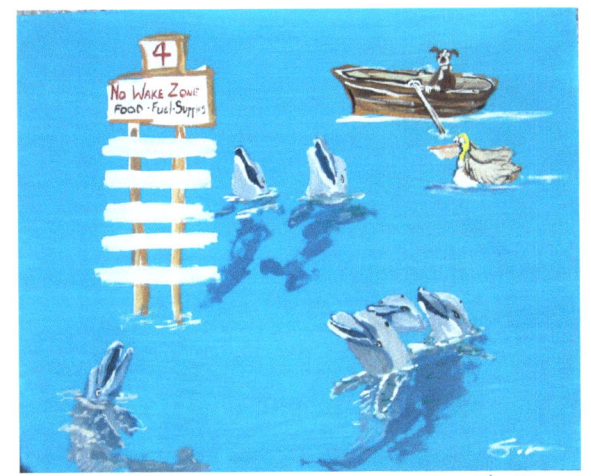

#198 Blank
boards & dolphins

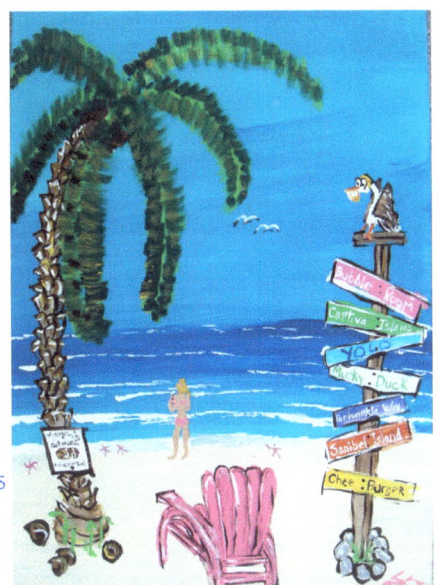

#246 Wendi on the Beach

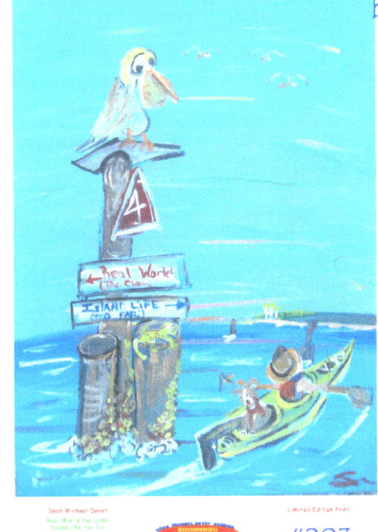

#203

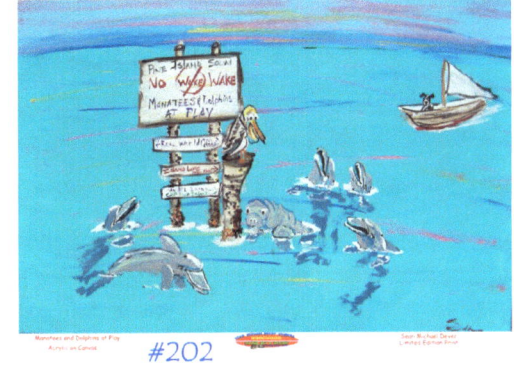

#202

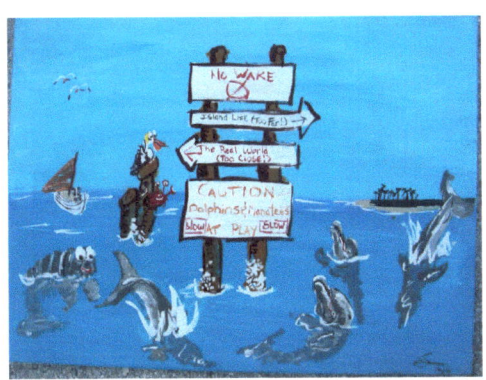

#244 Dolphins at play

Dolphin &
Manatee
at play... sunset

#208

Limited Edition
Print

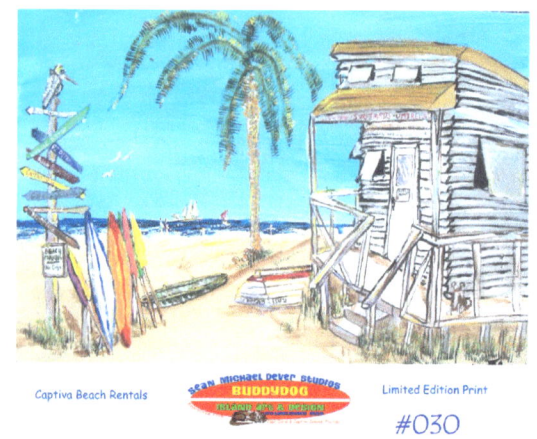

Captiva Beach Rentals   **BUDDYDOG**   Limited Edition Print

#030

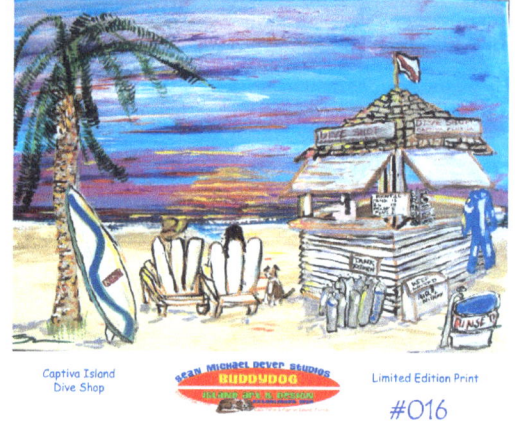

Captiva Island Dive Shop   **BUDDYDOG**   Limited Edition Print

#016

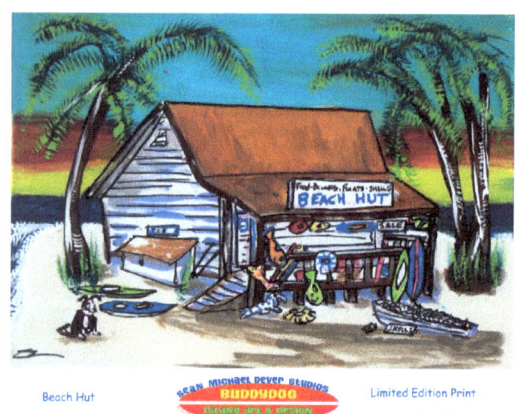

Beach Hut   **BUDDYDOG**   Limited Edition Print

#036

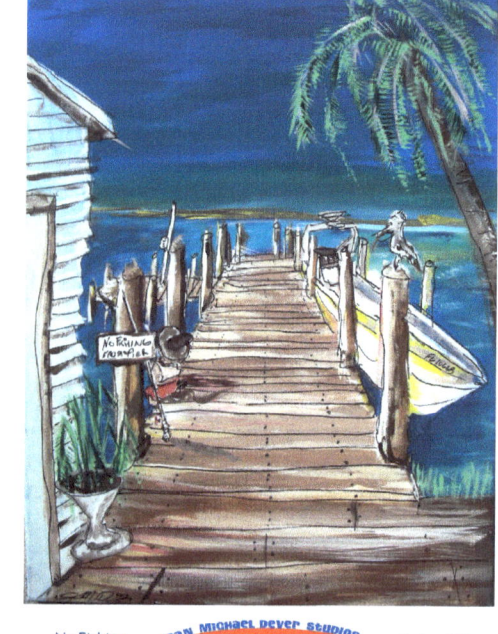

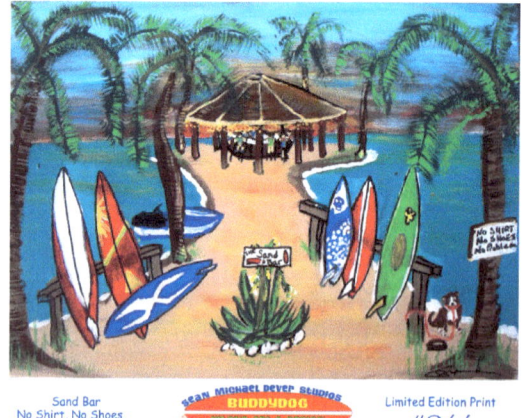

Sand Bar
No Shirt, No Shoes,
No Problem
    BUDDYDOG   Limited Edition Print

#044

No Fishing
From Pier #1
    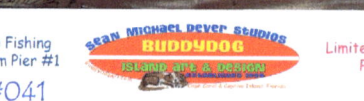   Limited Edition
Print

#041

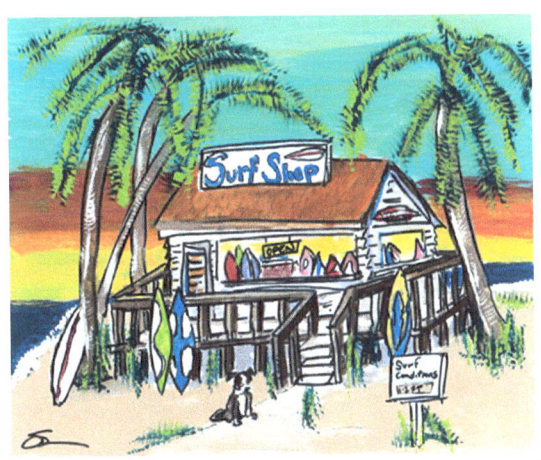

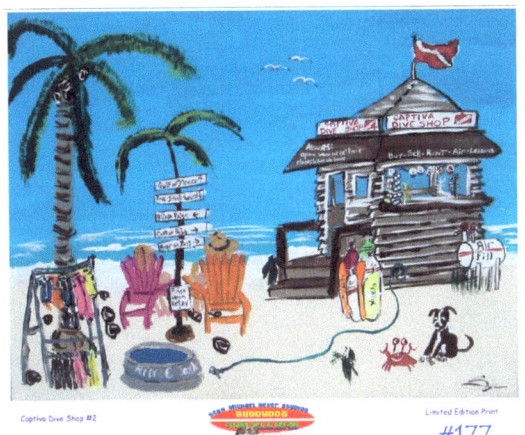

#133 Umbrellas & Chairs

#519 Surf Shop

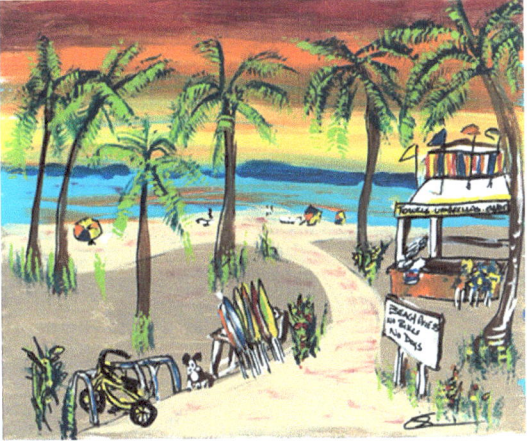

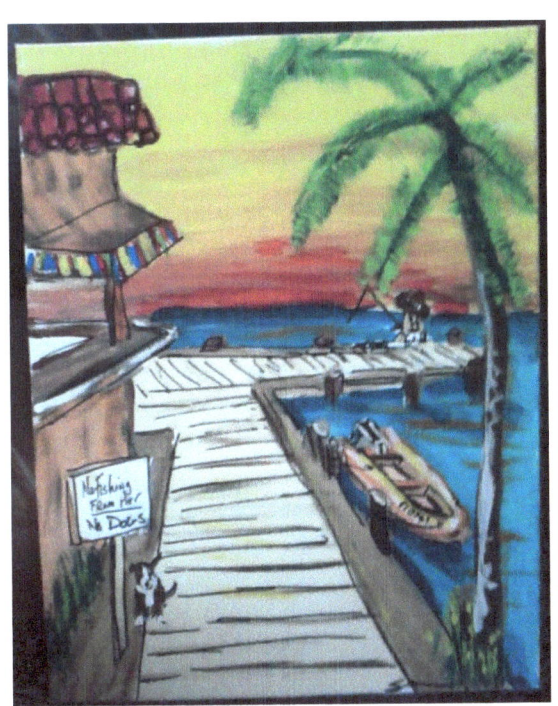

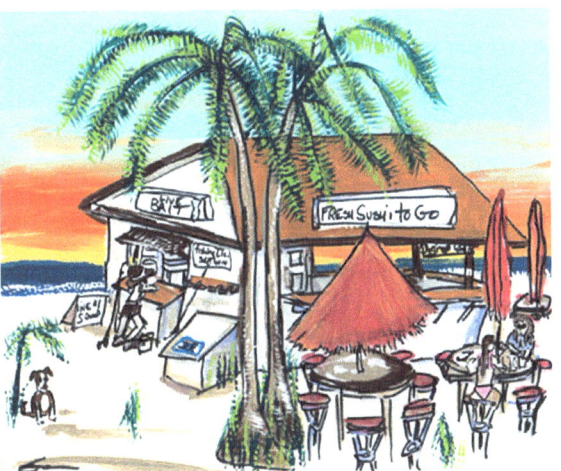

#140 Buddydog No Fishin on Pier No.2

#109 Live Bait & Sushi

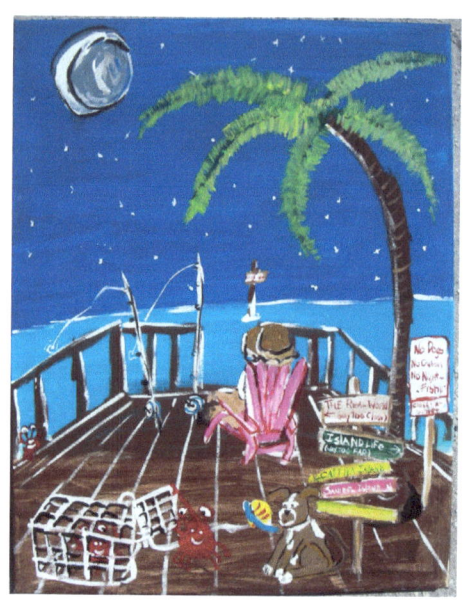

#257 Night Fishin'

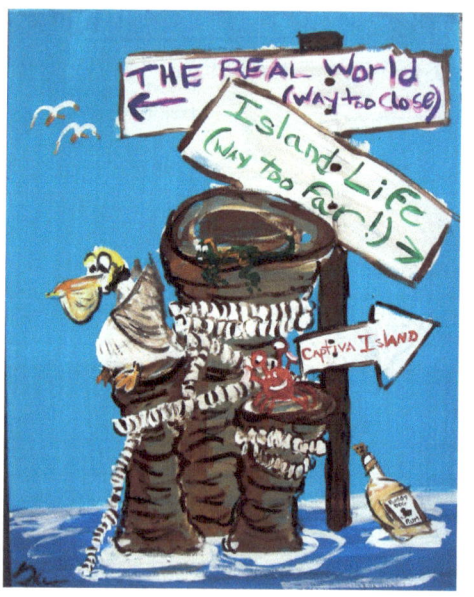

#258 Real World/Island Life

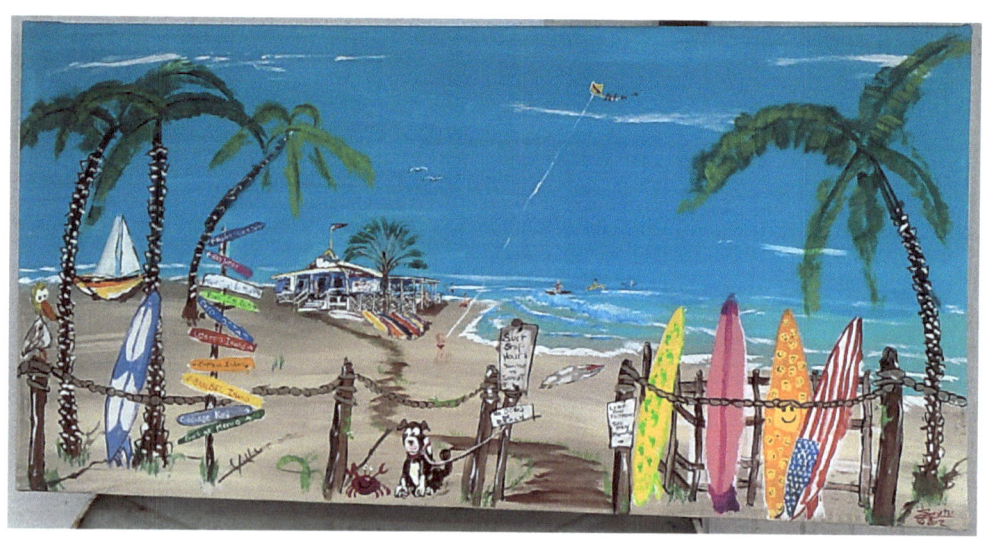

#253 Kite Flying & surf shop

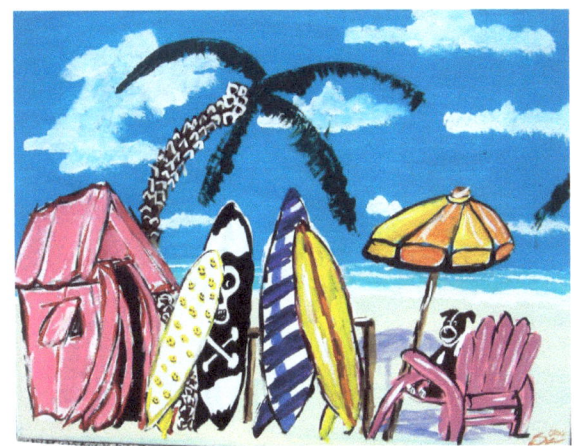

#256 Surfboards No.4

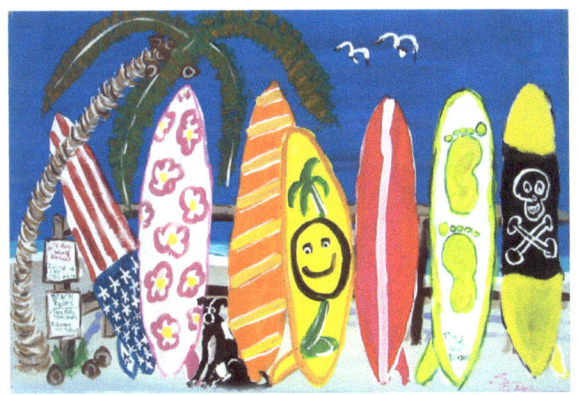

#263   Seven Surfboards

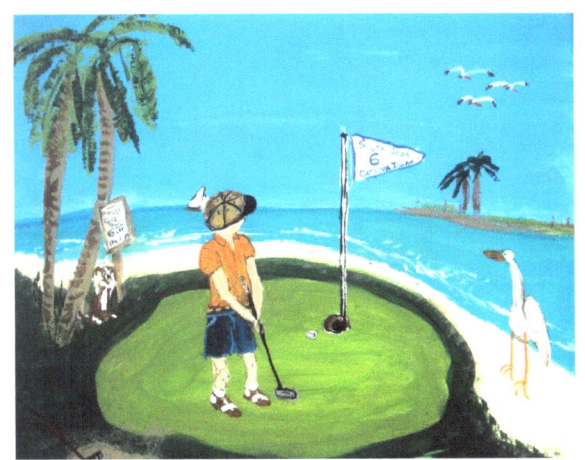

#329 South Seas Hole #6

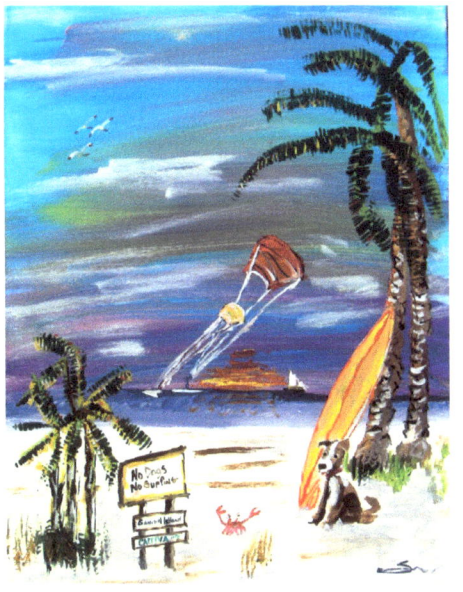

#510 Kite Surfing Captiva Sanibel

#537 Blind Pass Surfers

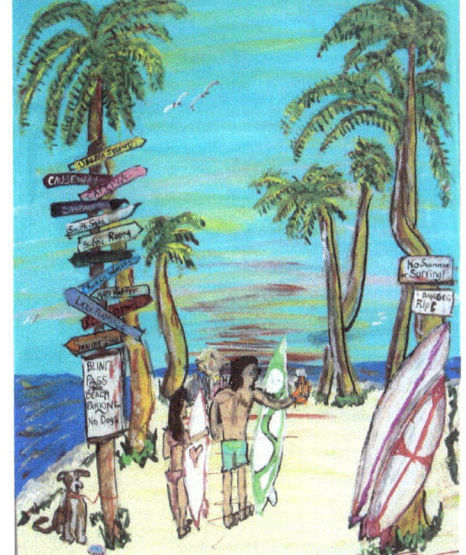

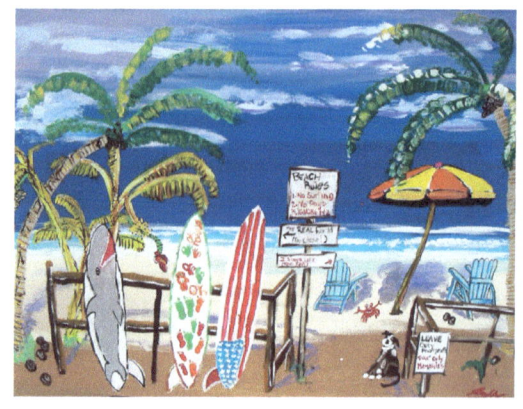

Beach Rules
acrylic on canvas

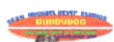

Limited Edition Print
#248

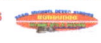

Sean Michael Dever - Acrylic on Canvas

Hot Air Balloons over Captiva

LIMITED EDITION PRINT
#252

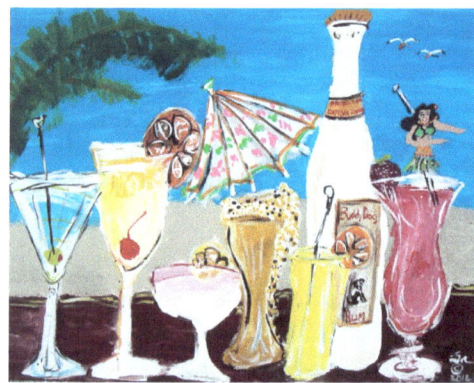

Sean Michael Dever 2012

Island Cocktails

Acrylic on Canvas

Limited Edition Print
#247

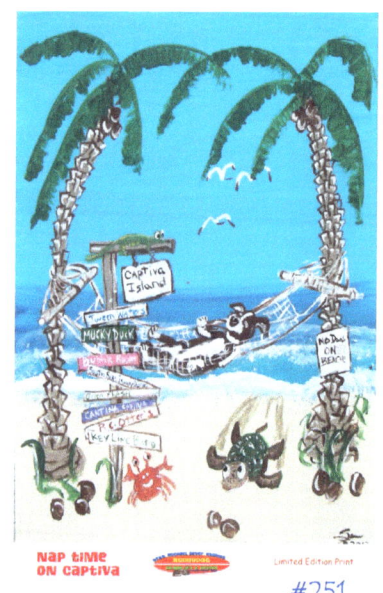

Nap Time on Captiva

Limited Edition Print
#251

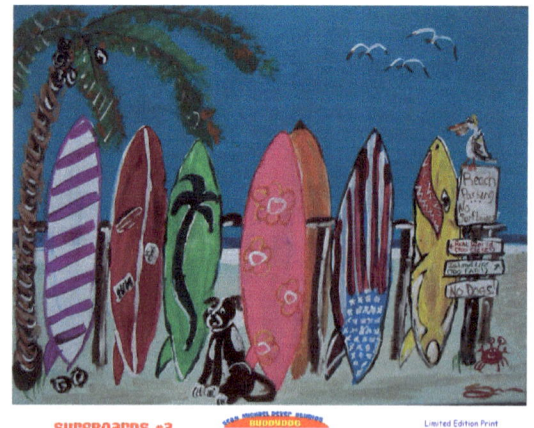

Surfboards #3

Limited Edition Print
#249

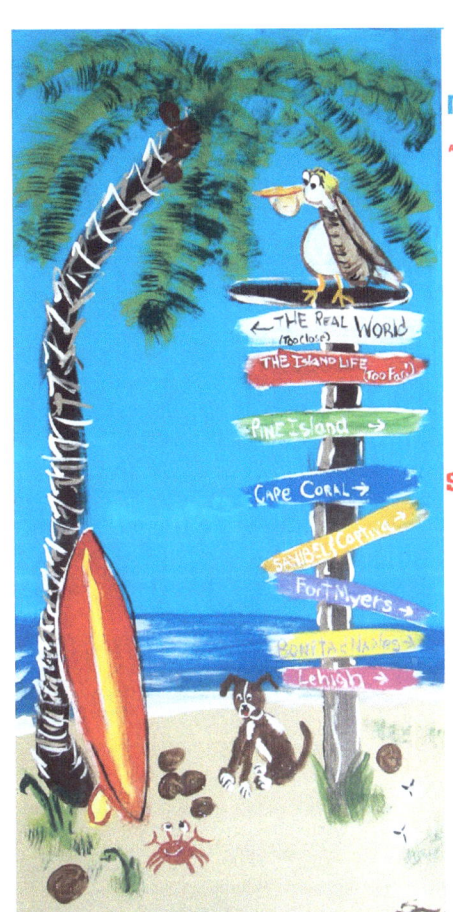

#217 Surfboard & signs

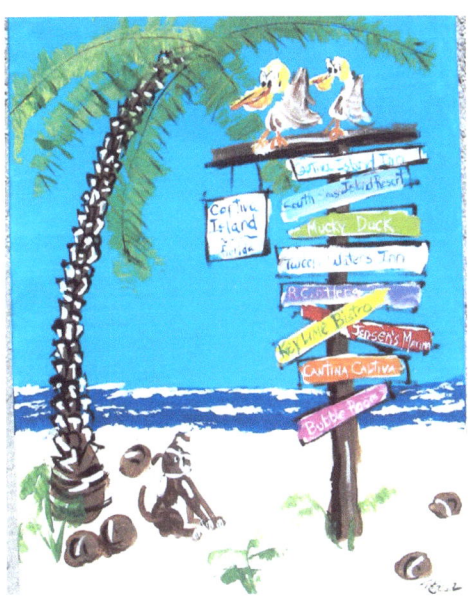

#259 Island Signs and Pelicans

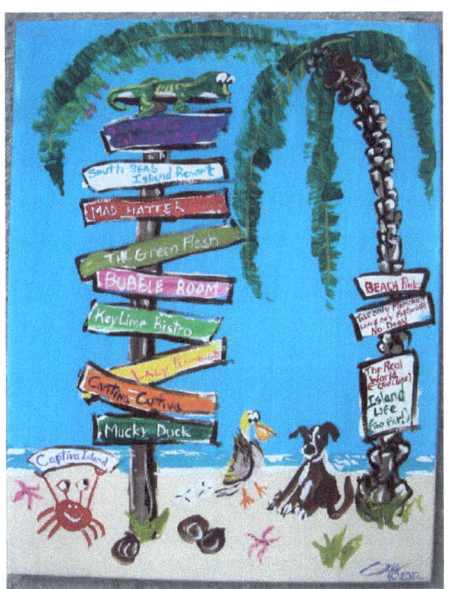

#254 Island signs

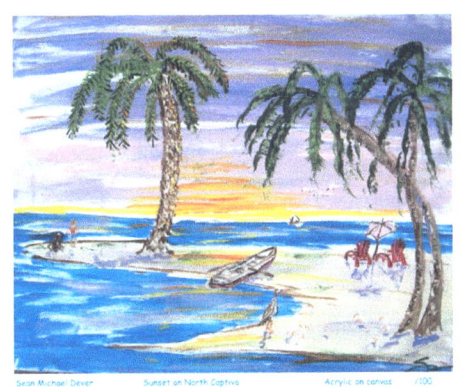

#088 Sunset on north captiva

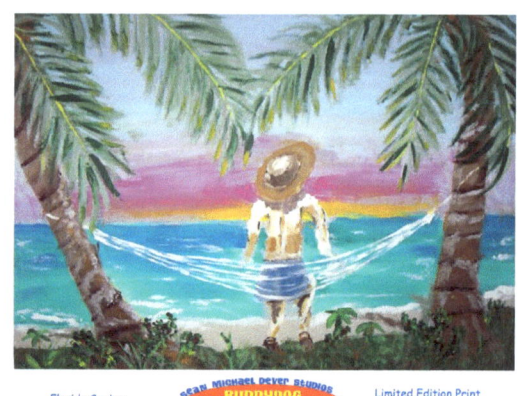

Florida Cowboy — BUDDYDOG — Limited Edition Print #033A

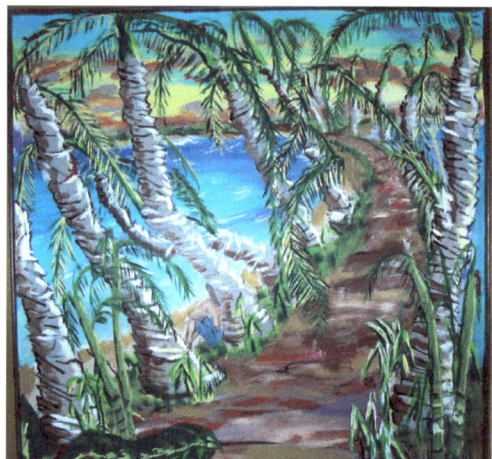

Pink Flip-Flops — BUDDYDOG — Limited Edition Print #057

#097
8 red geckos on the
causeway

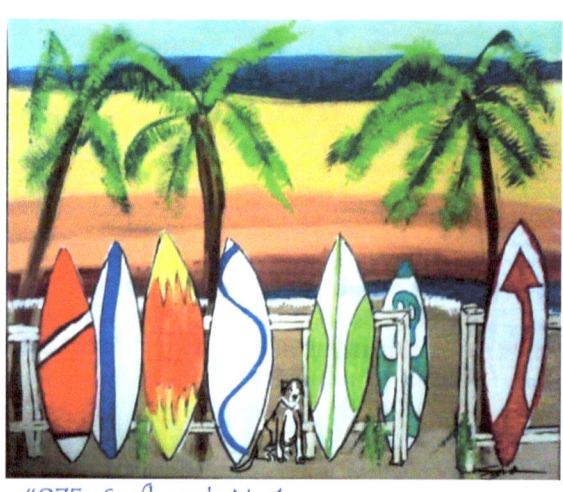

#056 Lighthouse

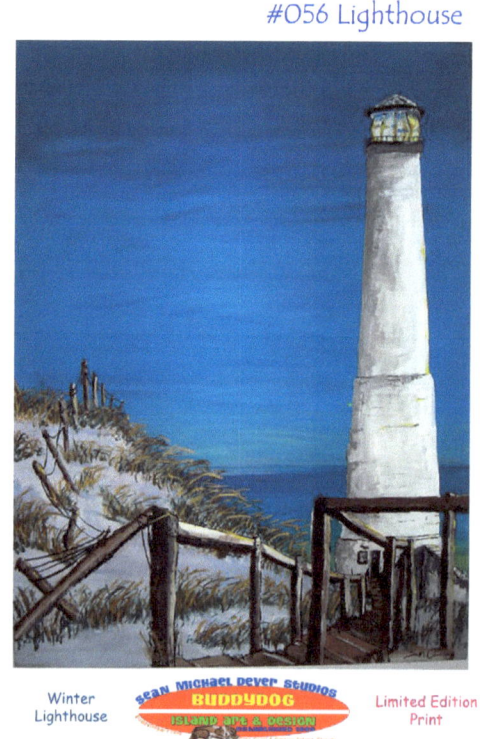

#075   Surfboards No.1

Winter Lighthouse — BUDDYDOG — Limited Edition Print

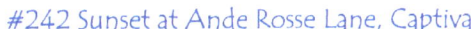

#242 Sunset at Ande Rosse Lane, Captiva

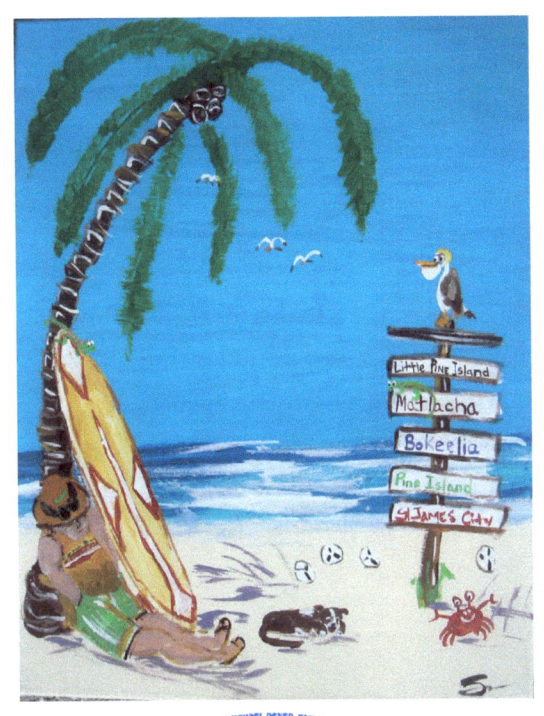

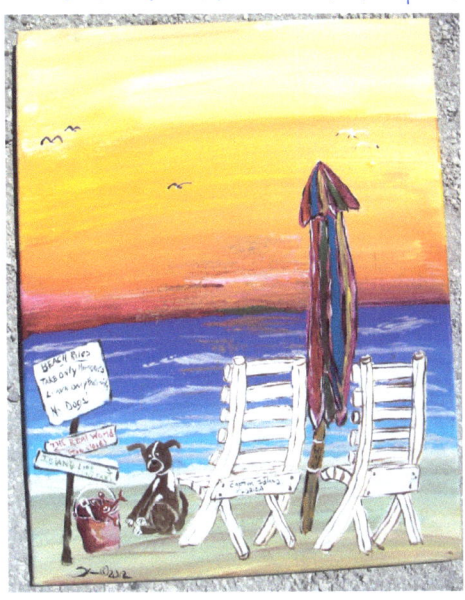

Nap Time #1  Limited Edition Print

#200

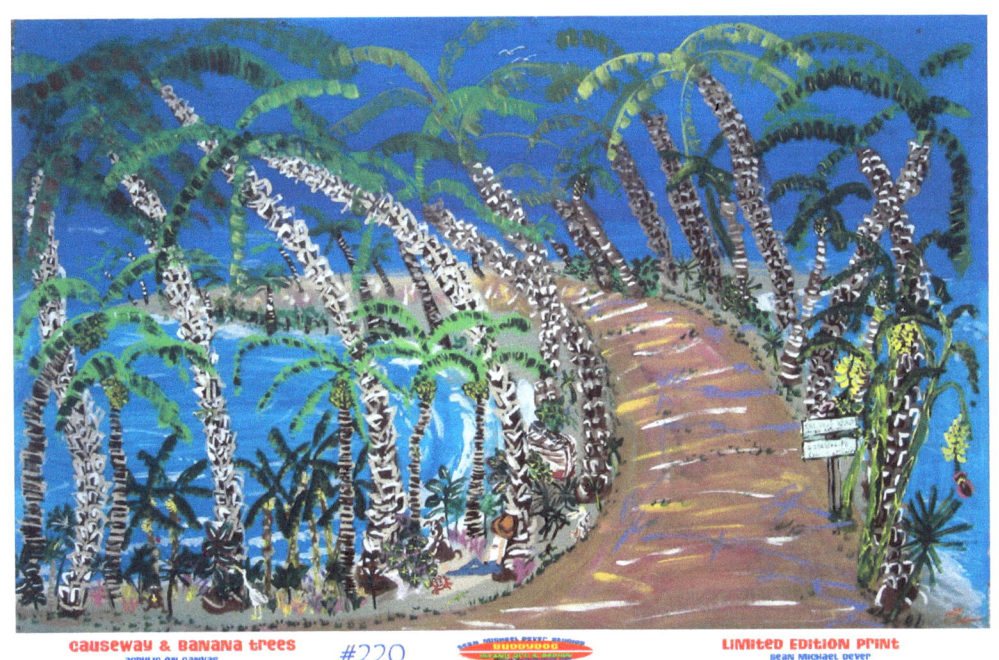

Causeway & Banana Trees #220 **Limited Edition Print**
acrylic on canvas   Sean Michael Dever

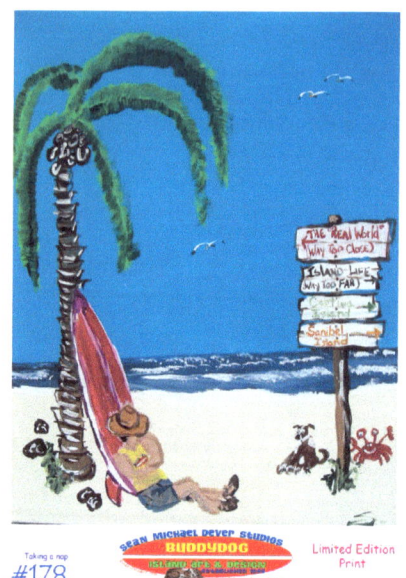

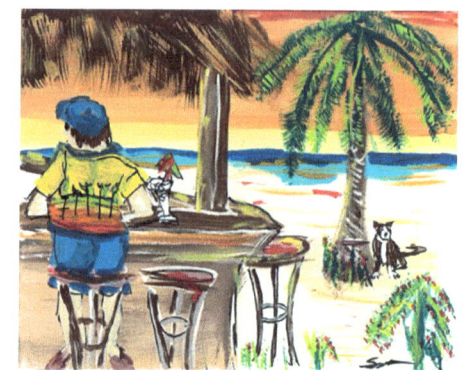

#134
Tiki Bar

Taking a nap

#178

Limited Edition Print

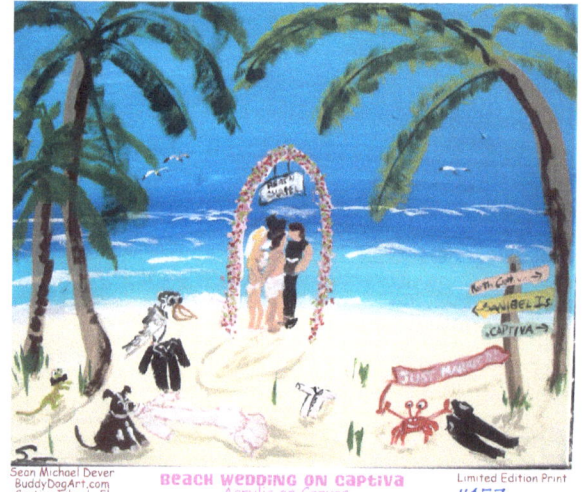

Sean Michael Dever
BuddyDogArt.com
Captiva Island , Fl

BEACH WEDDING ON CAPTIVA
Acrylic on Canvas

Limited Edition Print

#153

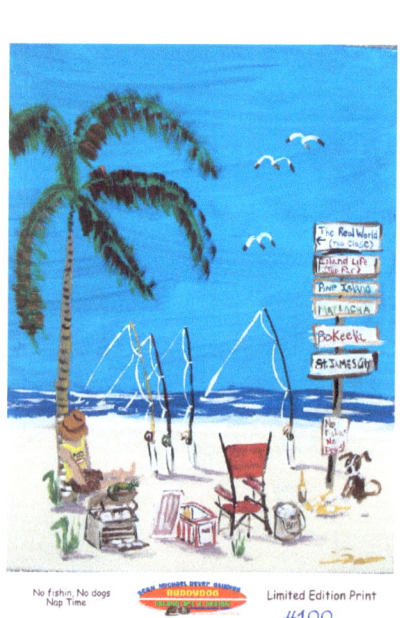

No fishin, No dogs
Nap Time

#199

Limited Edition Print

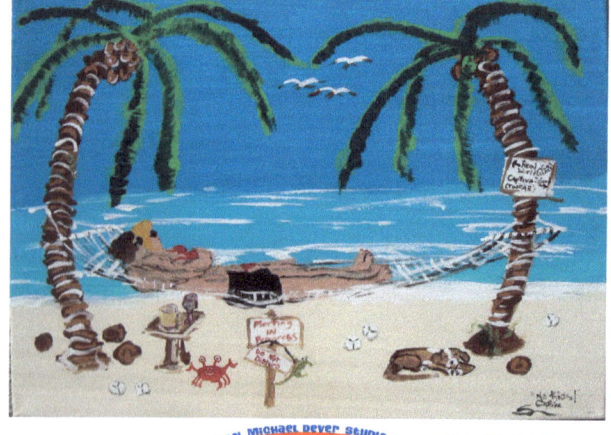

Do not disturb, No Kids

#173

Limited Edition Print

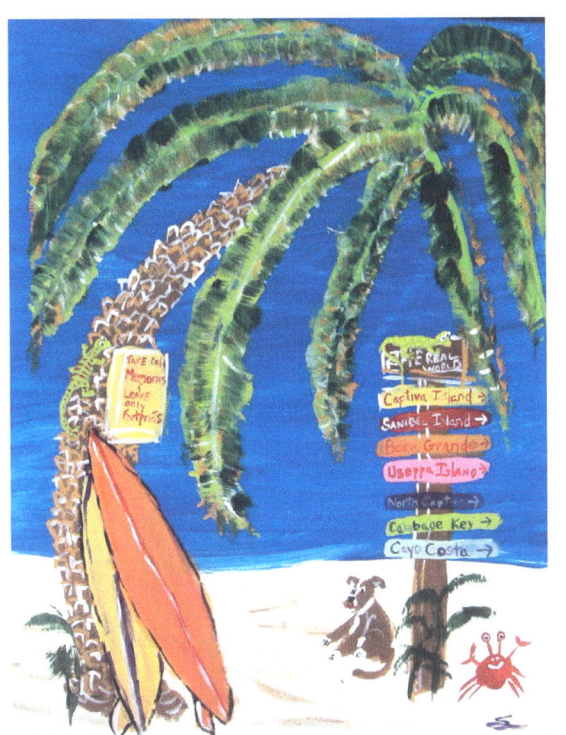

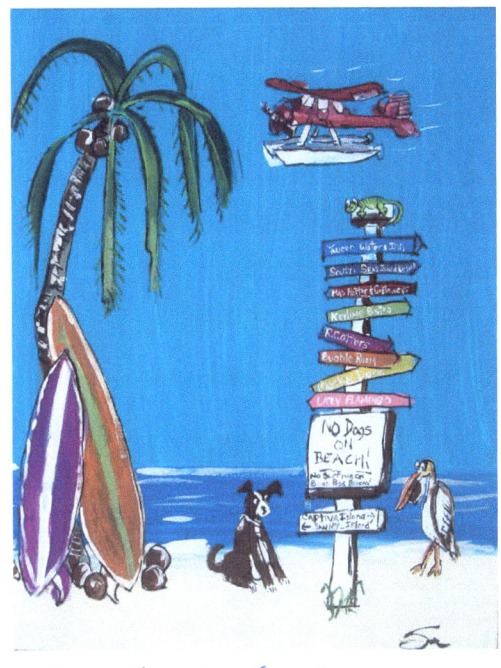

#150 Seaplane & surfboards

#144 The real world & all islands

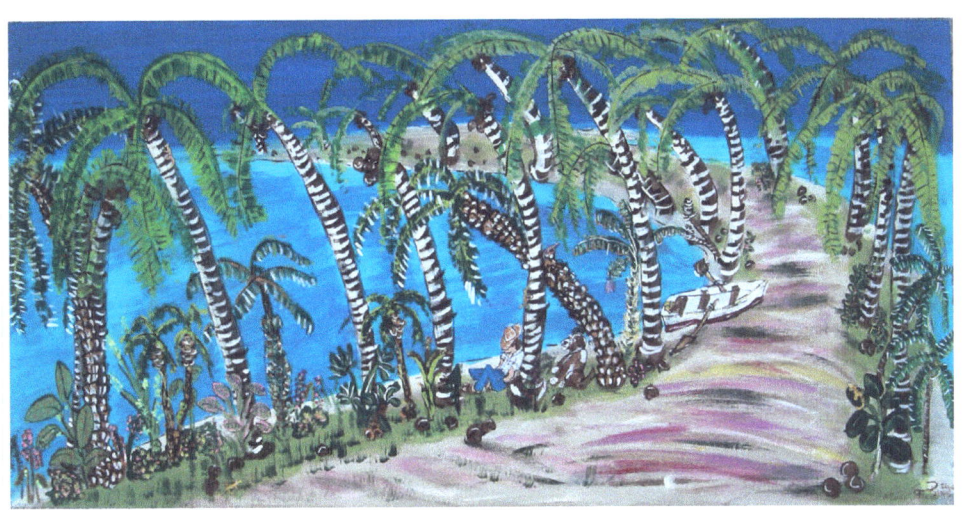

#147   A Dozen Lizards and a Frog on the Causeway

Sean Michael Dever
BuddyDogArt.com
Captiva Island, FL

Limited Edition Print

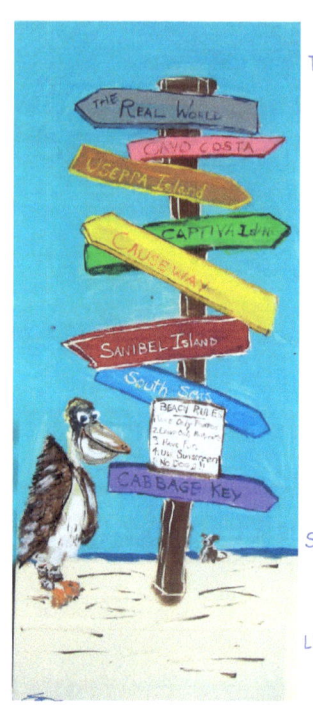

The Real World....
That Way
(2012)
Acrylic On
Canvas

Sean
Michael
Dever

Limited Edition
#102

#108 Sailboarding Sanibel

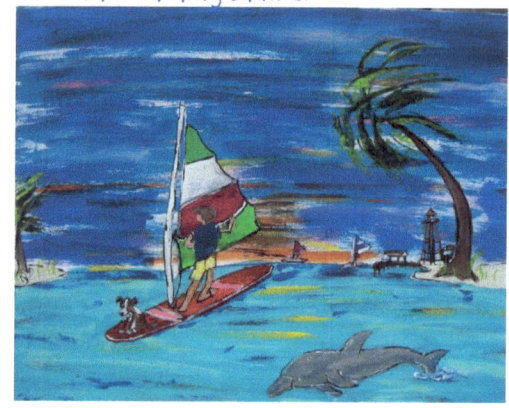

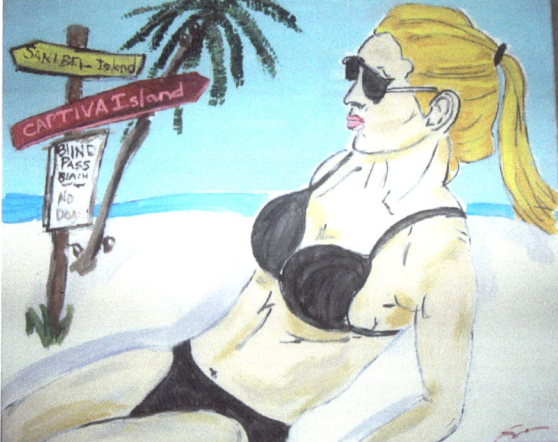

#125
Blonde on
the beach

#066 Blind Pass & Island Restaurants

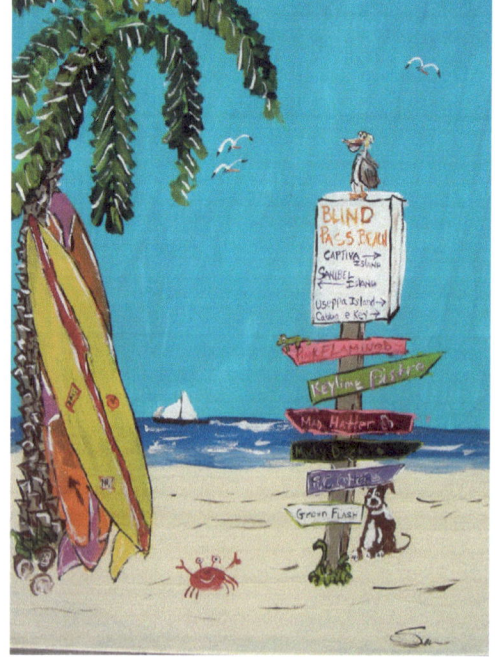

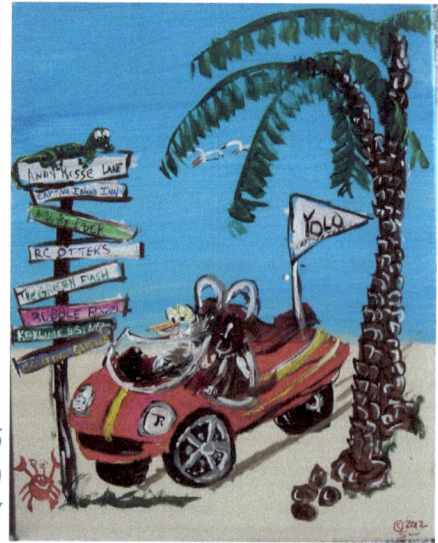

#135
Yolo Beach
Buggy

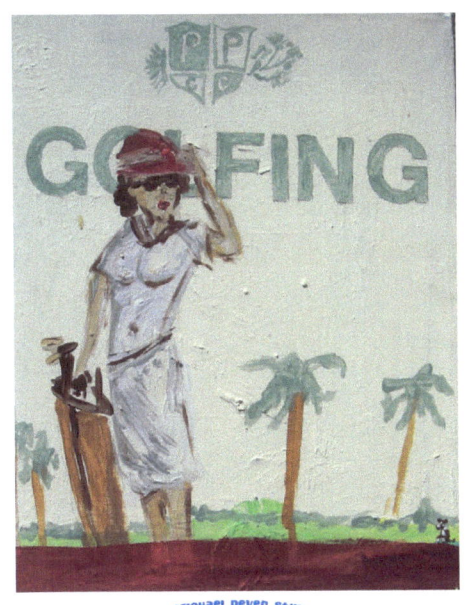

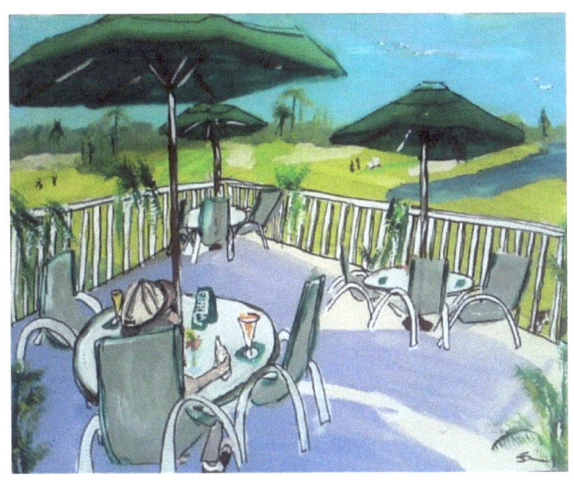

#103 The 19th Hole

#110
Women's
Golf

SEAN MICHAEL DEVER STUDIOS
BUDDYDOG
ISLAND ART & DESIGN

Limited Edition
Print

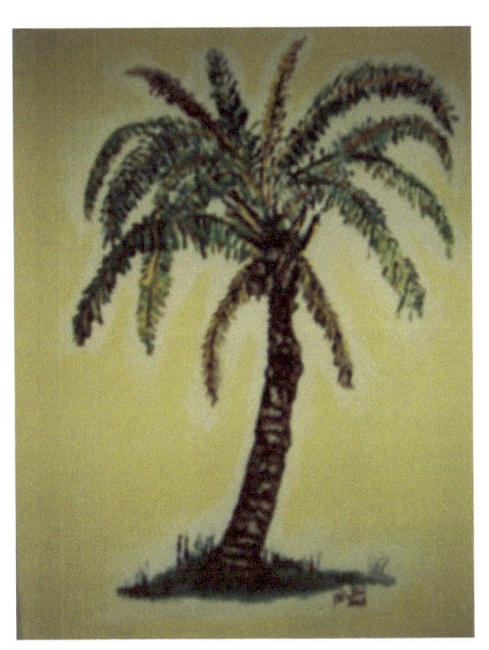

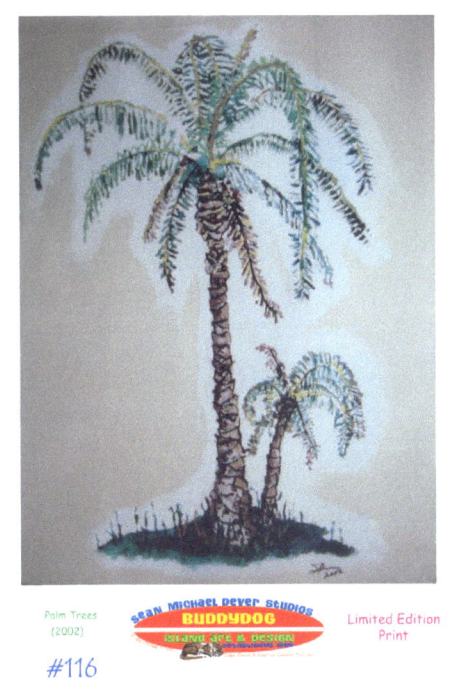

Palm Trees
(2002)

SEAN MICHAEL DEVER STUDIOS
BUDDYDOG
ISLAND ART & DESIGN

Limited Edition
Print

#116

PALM TREE

SEAN MICHAEL DEVER STUDIOS
BUDDYDOG

Limited Edition Print

#117

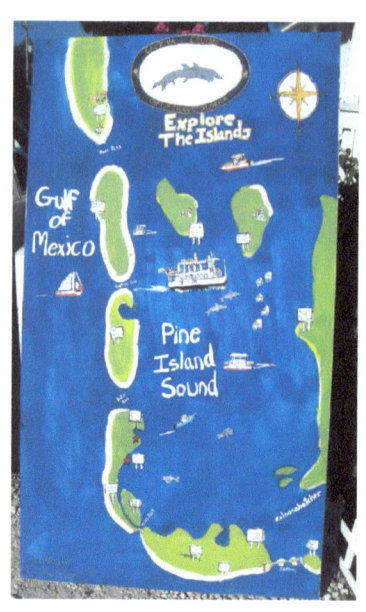

#111 Map of the Islands #3 Captiva Cruises

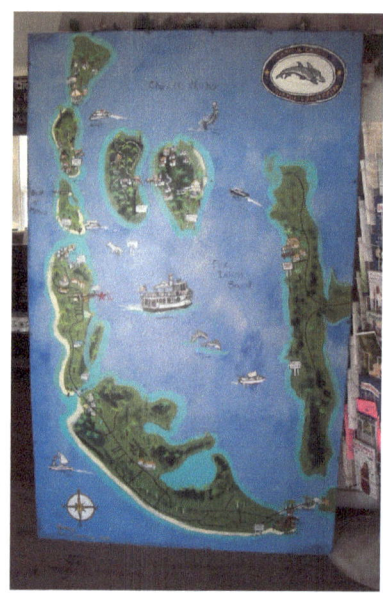

#124 Map of The Islands #1 Captiva Crusies

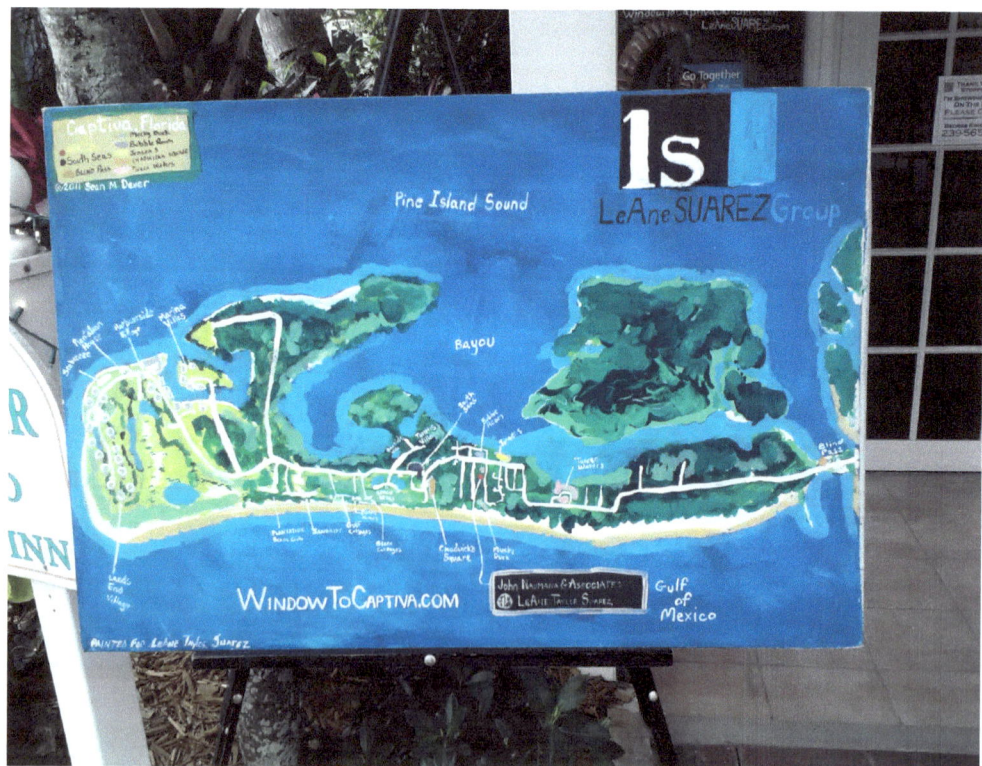

#123 Map of Captiva for LeAne Suarez Group

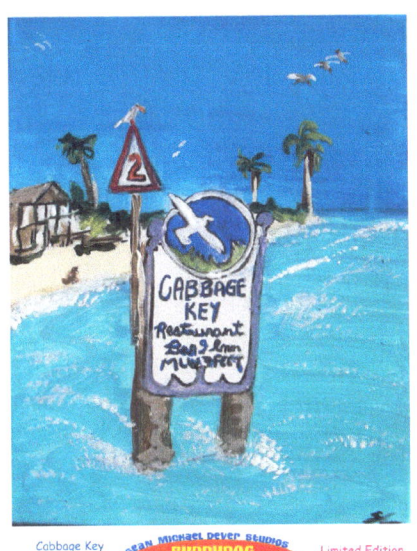

Cabbage Key
Marine Marker
Pine Island Sound, FL

Limited Edition
Print

#001

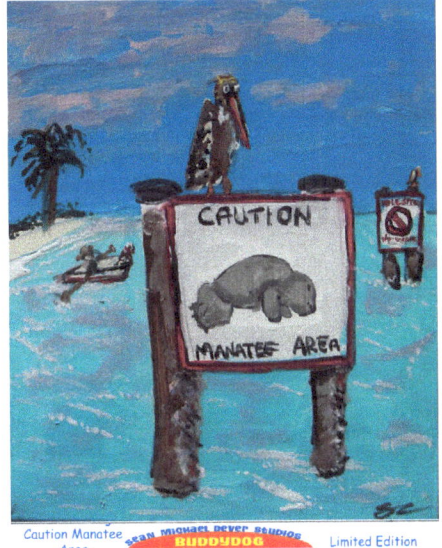

Caution Manatee
Area
Captiva, FL

Limited Edition
Print

#007

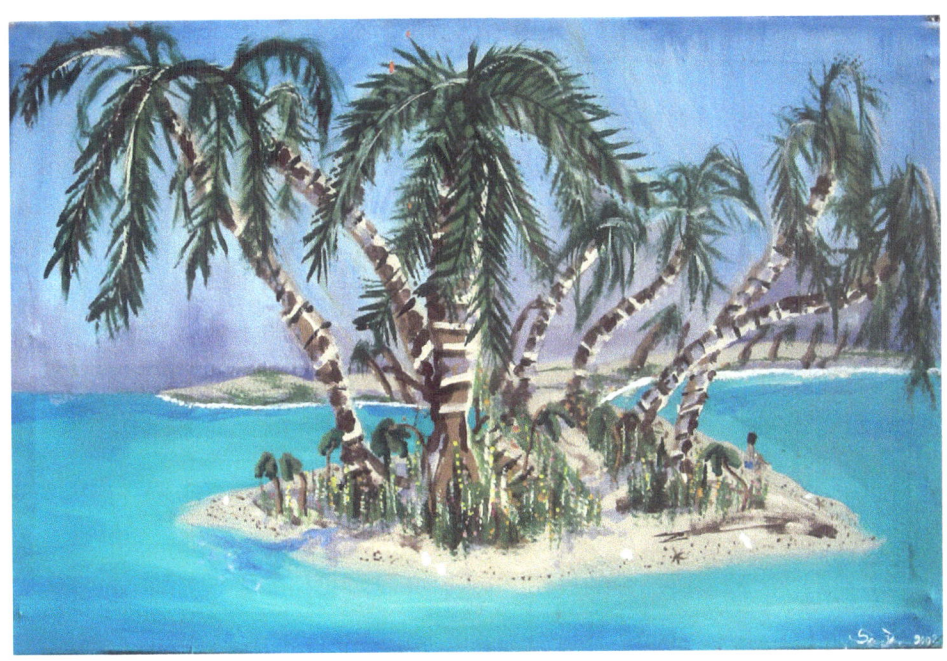

Alone at Lands End
Captiva

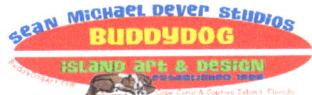

Limited Edition Print

#004

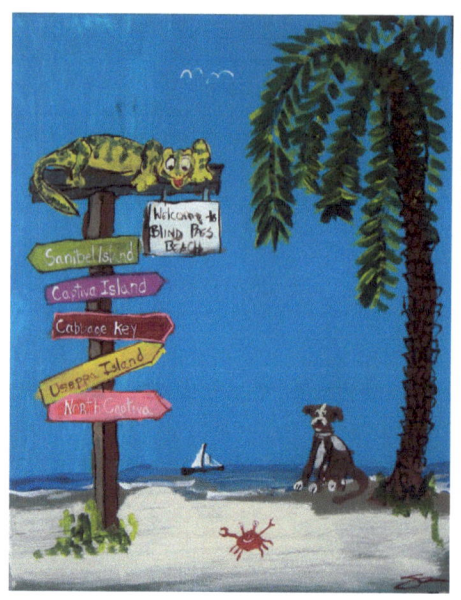

#068
Chameleon
at Blind
Pass
& Island
Restaurants

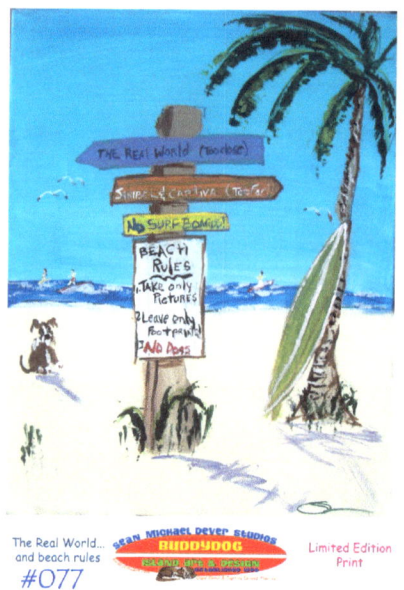

The Real World...
and beach rules
#077

Limited Edition
Print

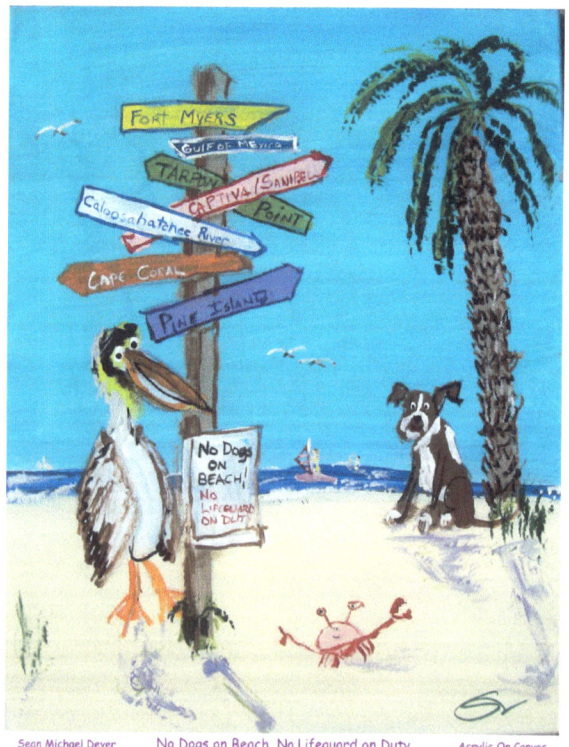

Sean Michael Dever   No Dogs on Beach, No Lifeguard on Duty   Acrylic On Canvas
#082

Blind Pass, Captiva
Surfers
#017

Limited Edition
Print

44

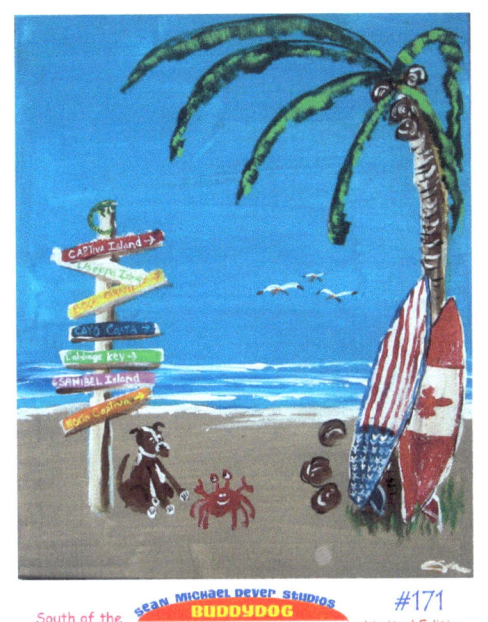

South of the
Border

#171

BUDDYDOG
SEAN MICHAEL DEVER STUDIOS
ISLAND ART & DESIGN

Limited Edition
Print

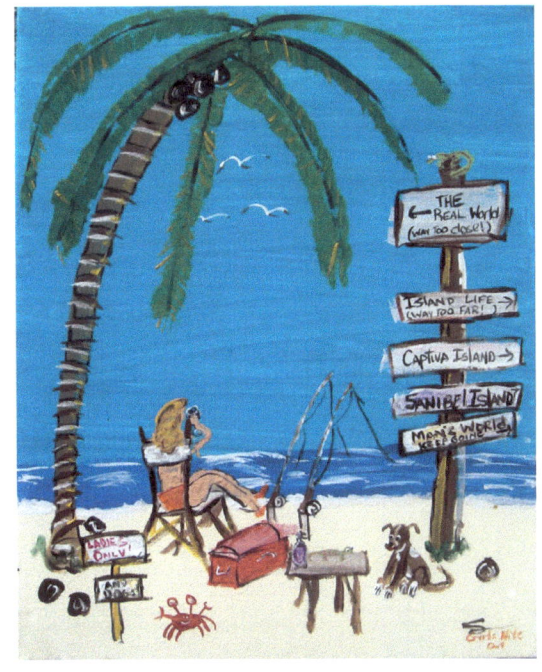

Girls Nite Out

#169

BUDDYDOG
SEAN MICHAEL DEVER STUDIOS
ISLAND ART & DESIGN

Limited Edition
Print

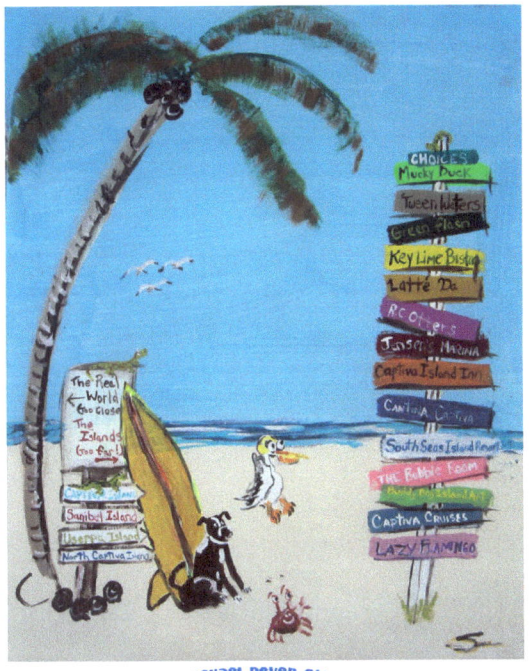

Island
Choices

#179

BUDDYDOG
SEAN MICHAEL DEVER STUDIOS
ISLAND ART & DESIGN

Limited Edition
Print

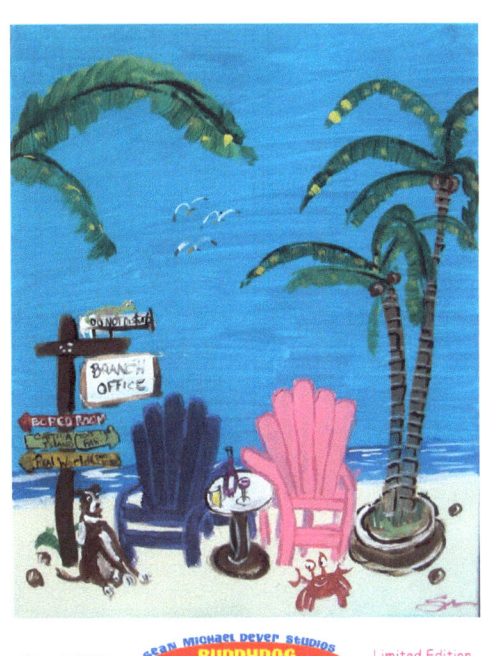

Branch Office

#168

BUDDYDOG
SEAN MICHAEL DEVER STUDIOS
ISLAND ART & DESIGN

Limited Edition
Print

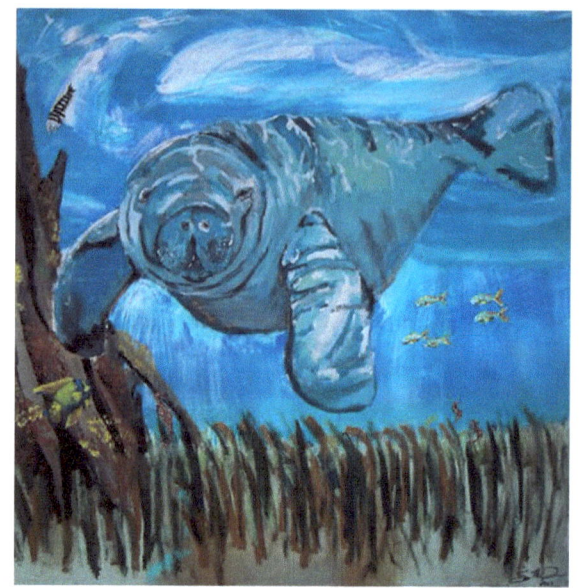

#032

Manatee #1

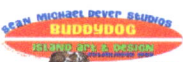

Limited Edition Print

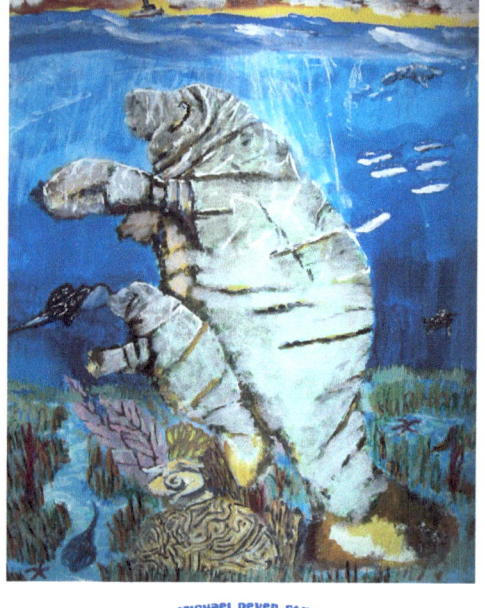

Manatee & Calf

#027

Limited Edition Print

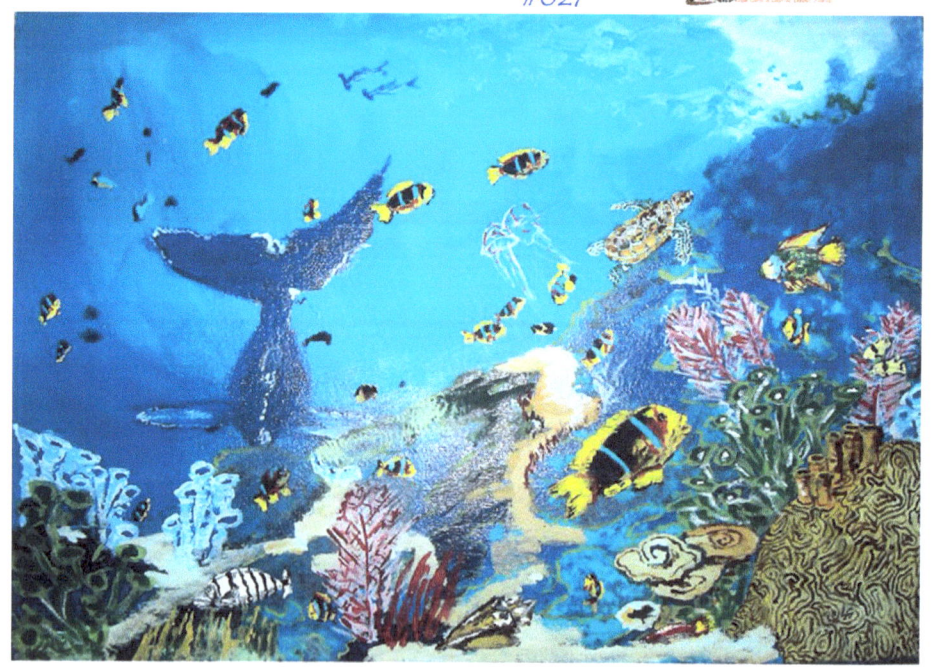

Coral Reef #1

#014

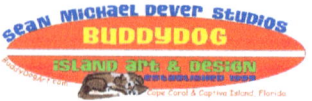

Limited Edition Print

46

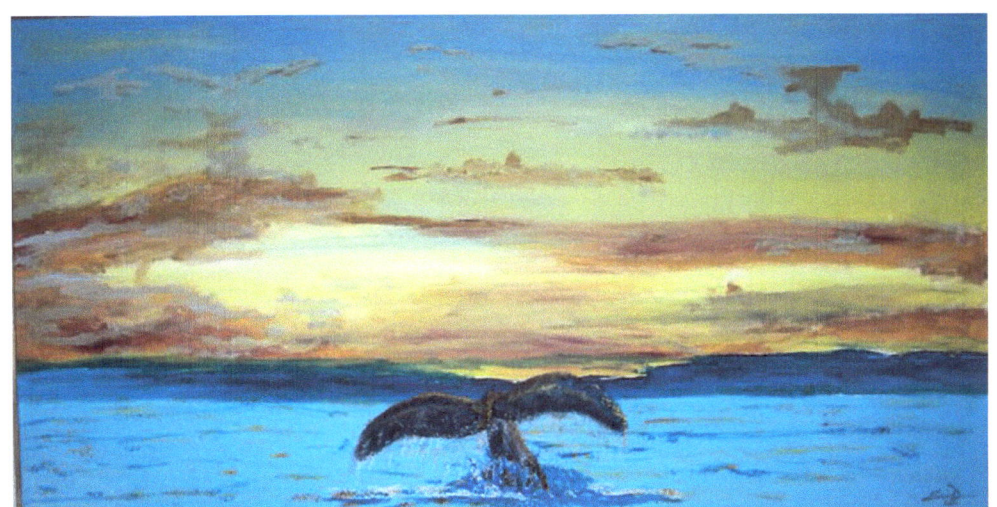

#071 Whale Tail

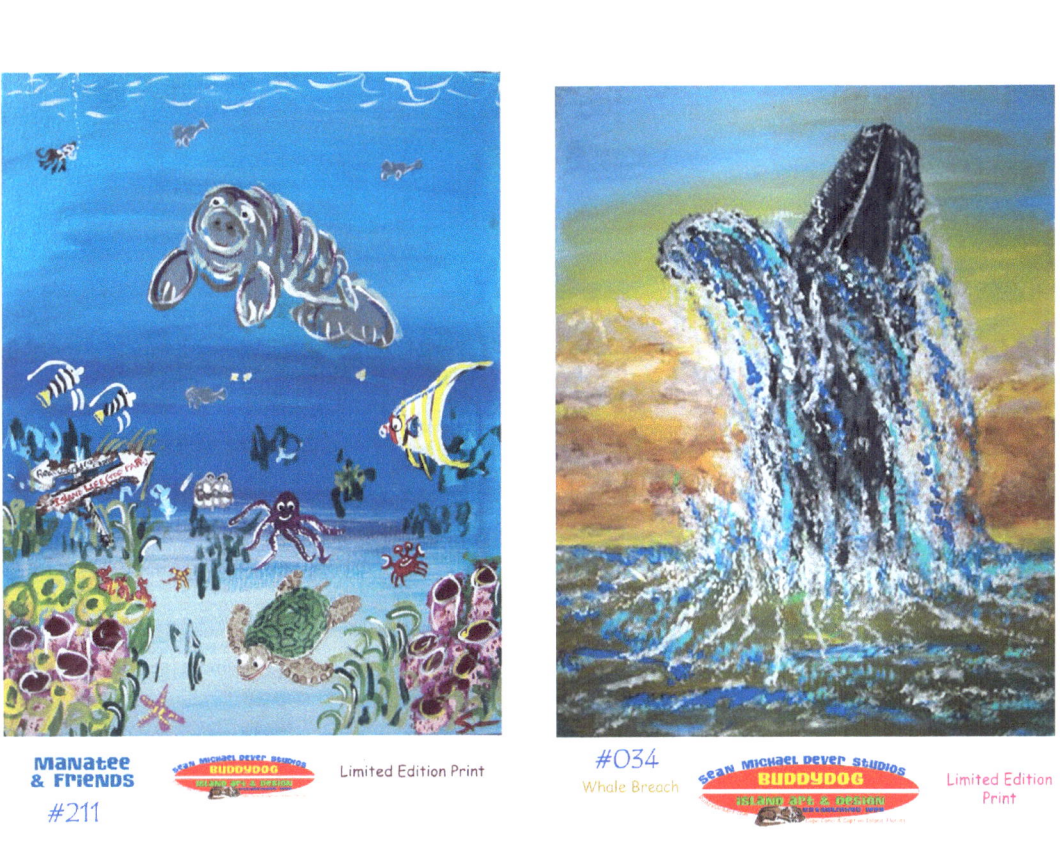

Manatee & Friends

#211

Limited Edition Print

#034

Whale Breach

Limited Edition Print

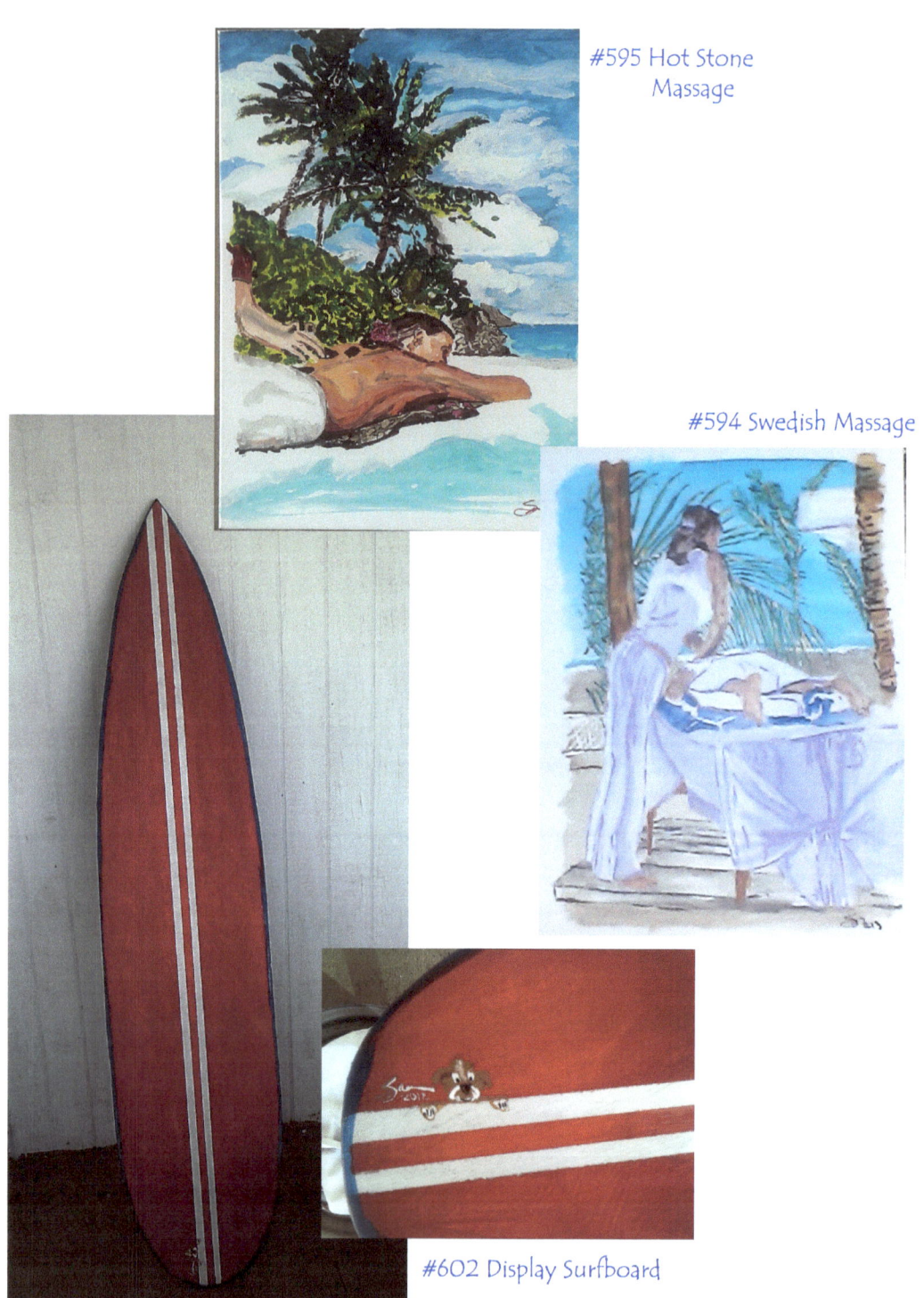

#595 Hot Stone
Massage

#594 Swedish Massage

#602 Display Surfboard

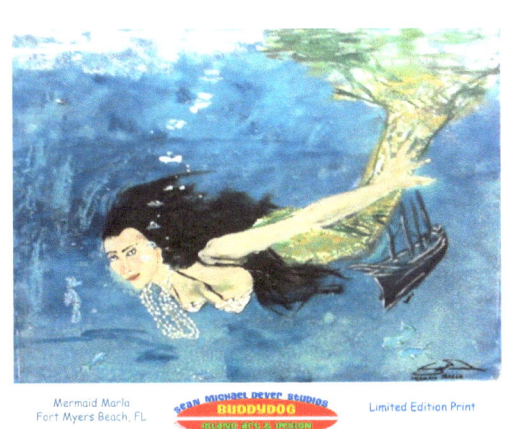

Mermaid Marla
Fort Myers Beach, FL

#054

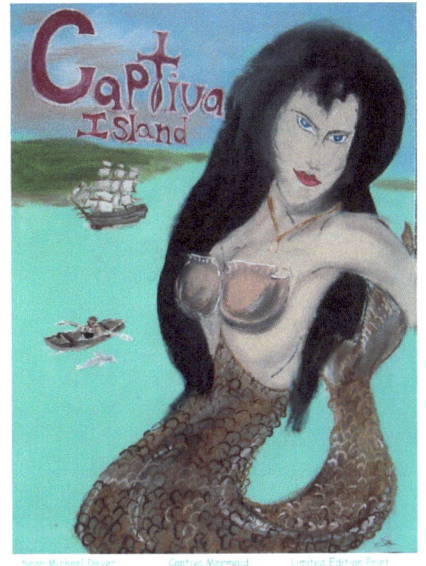

Sean Michael Dever   Captiva Mermaid   Limited Edition Print

#064

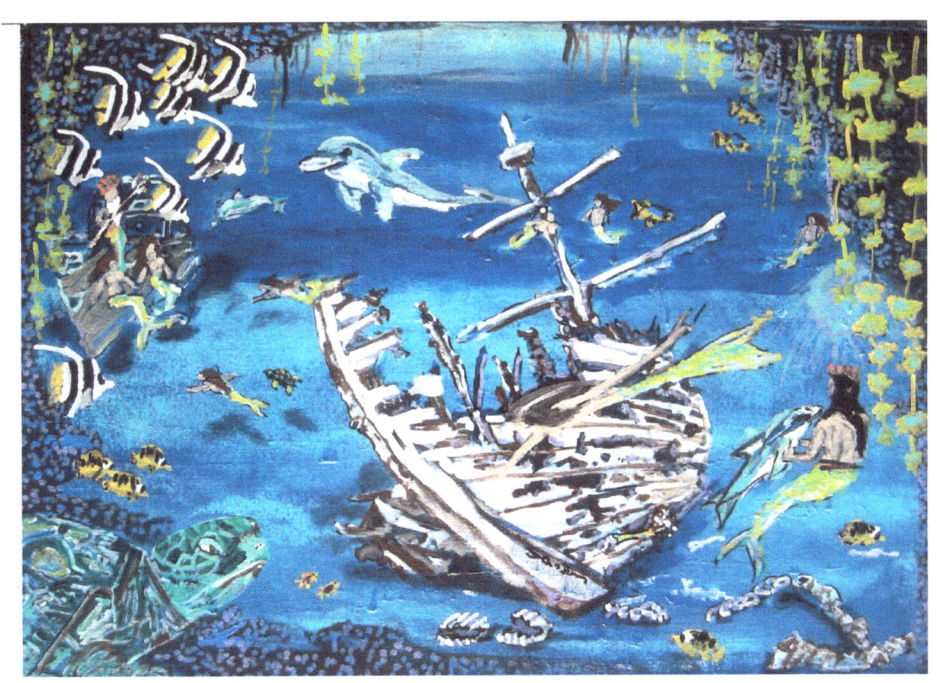

Royal Court of
Mermaids

#038

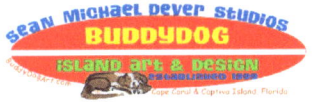

Limited Edition Print

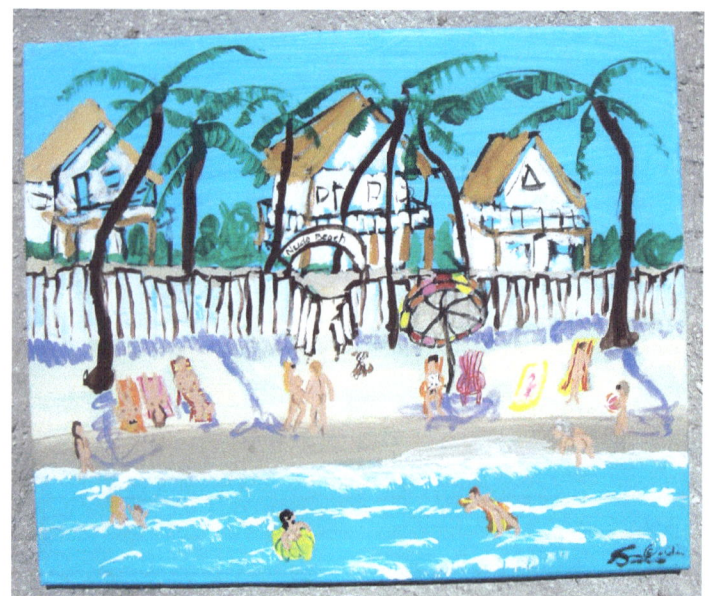

#255
Nude Beach
No.2

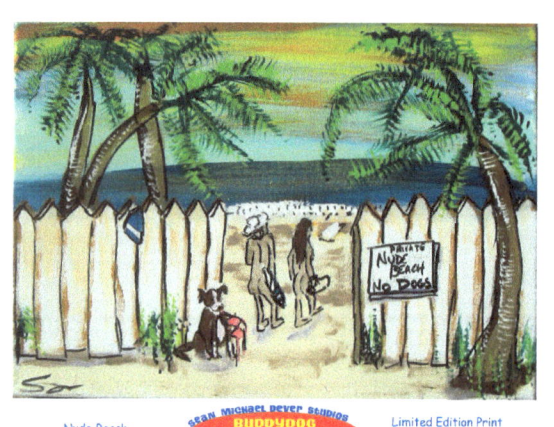

Nude Beach

#028

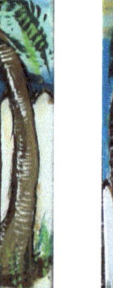

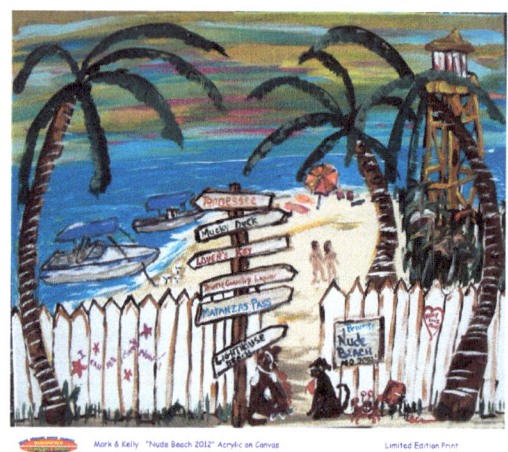

Mark & Kelly "Nude Beach 2012" Acrylic on Canvas   Limited Edition Print

#175

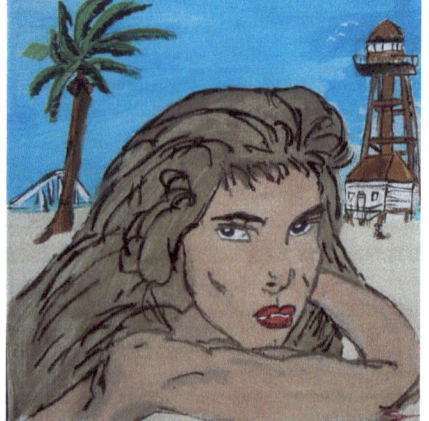

#328 Blonde at
Sanibel Lighthouse

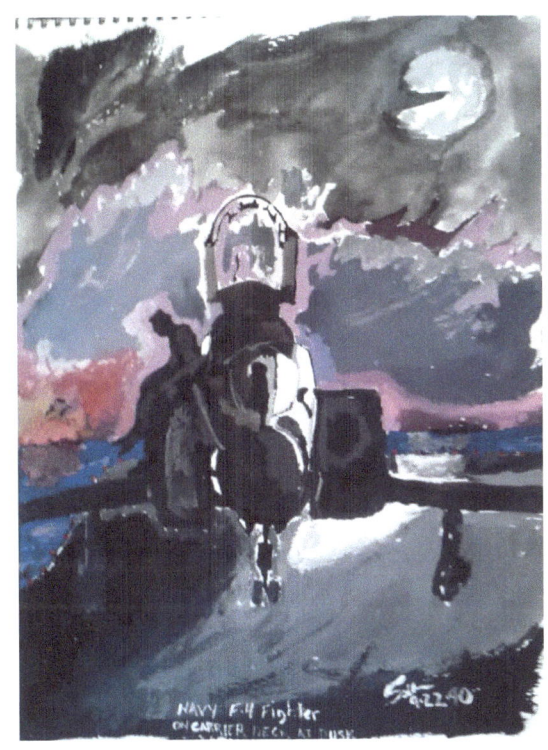

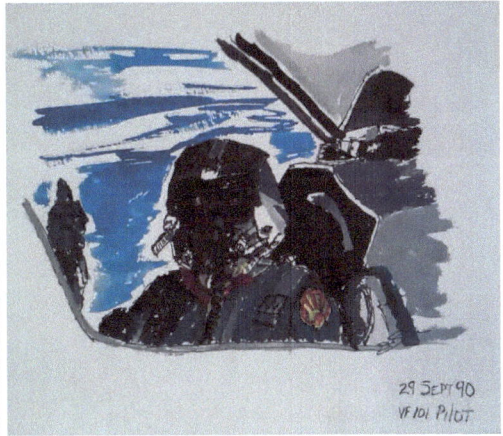

#979 Fighter Pilot

#978 US Navy F-4B Phantom

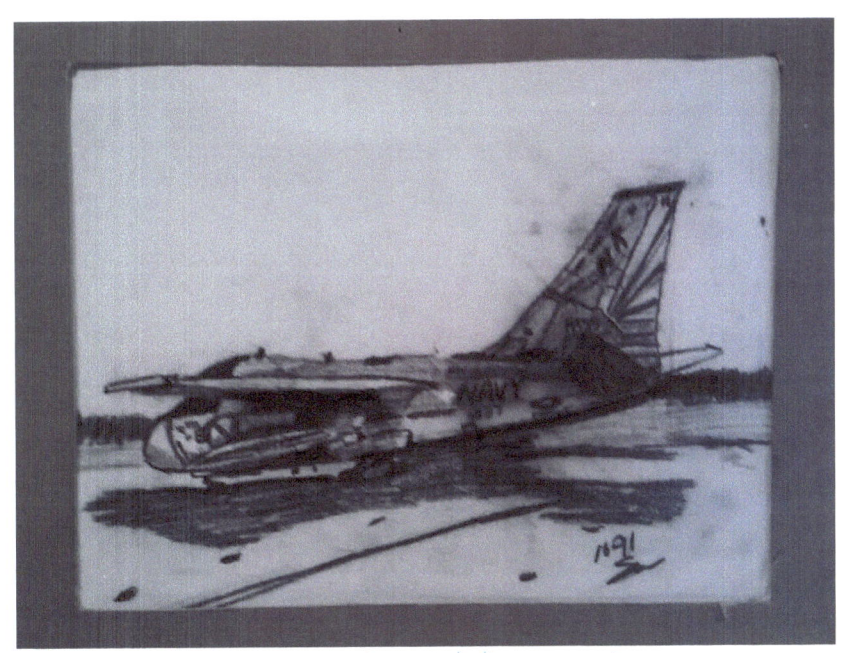

#980 US Navy S-3A Viking (Chalk on paper)

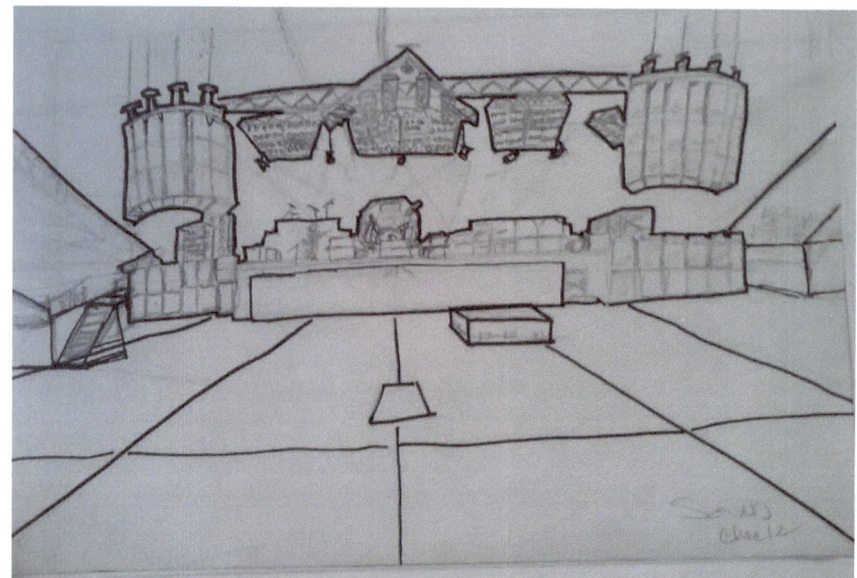

#970 Stagecraft

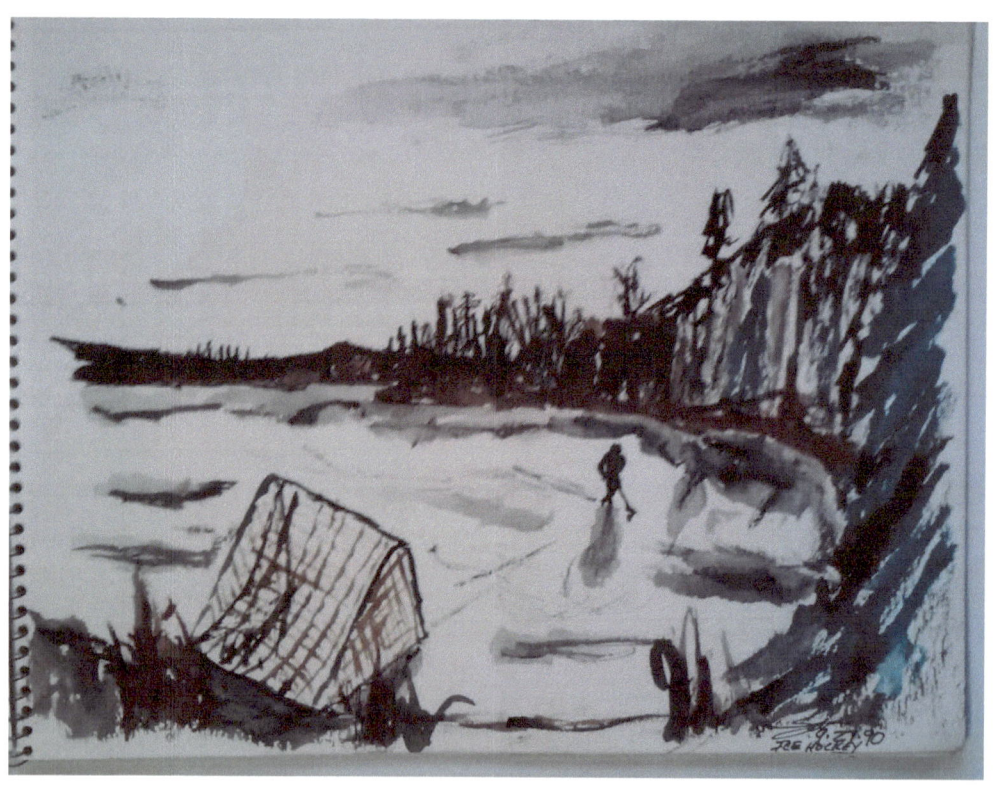

#972 Frozen lake in the Pocono Mountains

real places

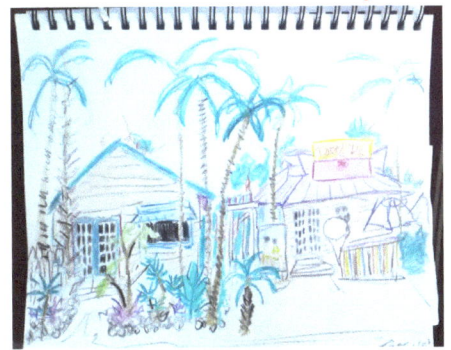

Original sketch of Latte Da & Captiva Island Inn
Captiva Island, Floriida   #821A

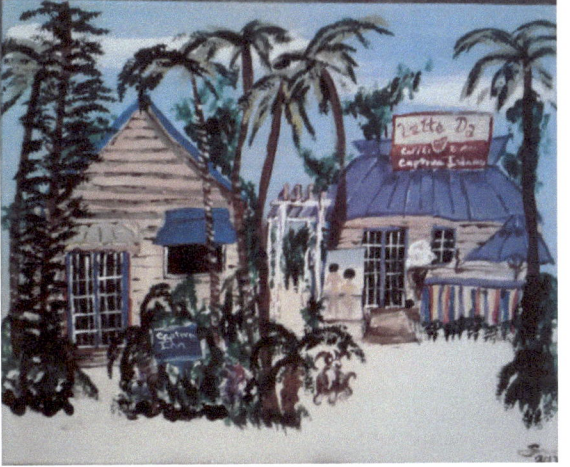

Latte Da & Captiva Island Inn...acrylic on canvas 16x20
(2013) #821

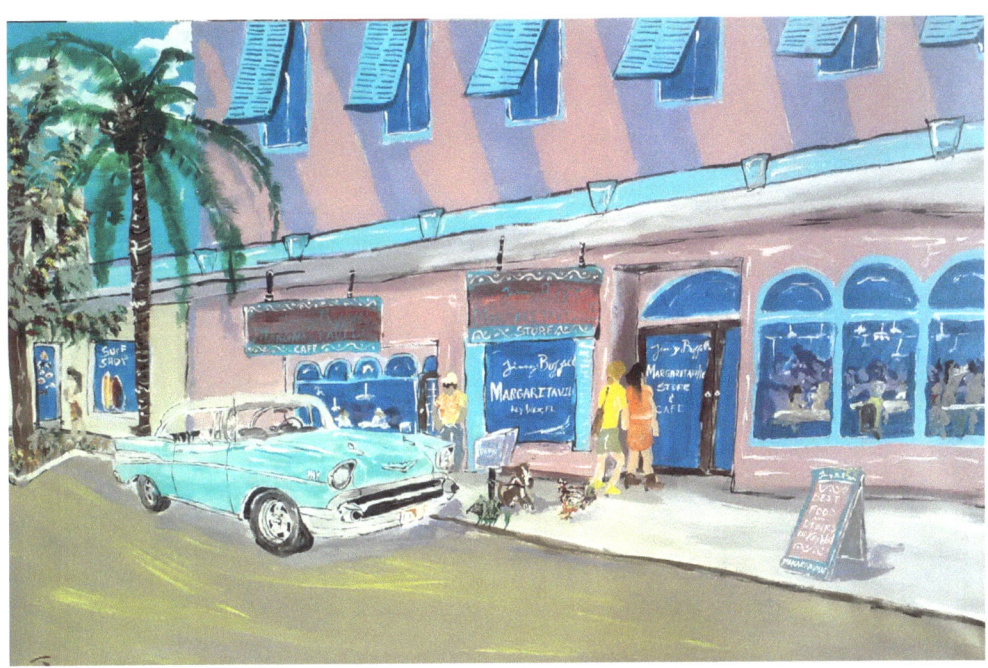

#598 Margarittaville, Key West – acrylic on canvas – 36x48 (2014)

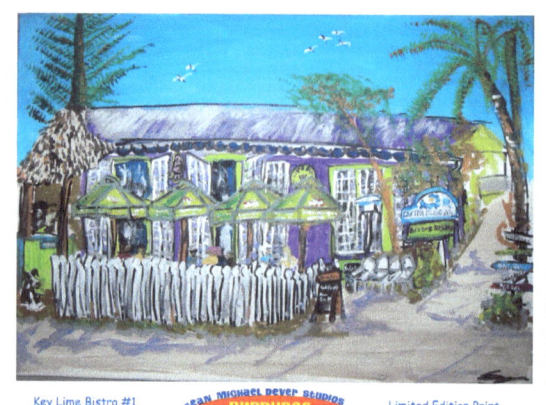

Key Lime Bistro #1
Captiva, FL

Limited Edition Print

#009

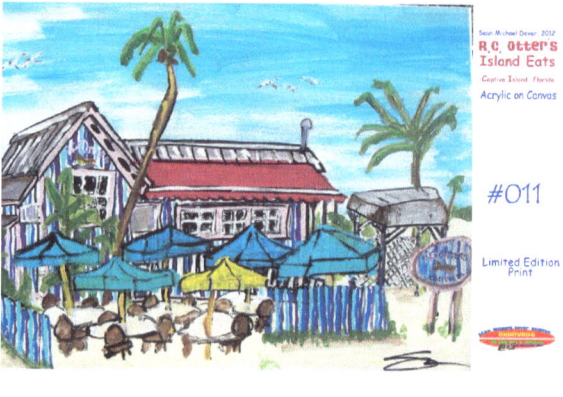

Sean Michael Dever 2012
R.C. Otter's
Island Eats
Captiva Island, Florida
Acrylic on Canvas

#011

Limited Edition
Print

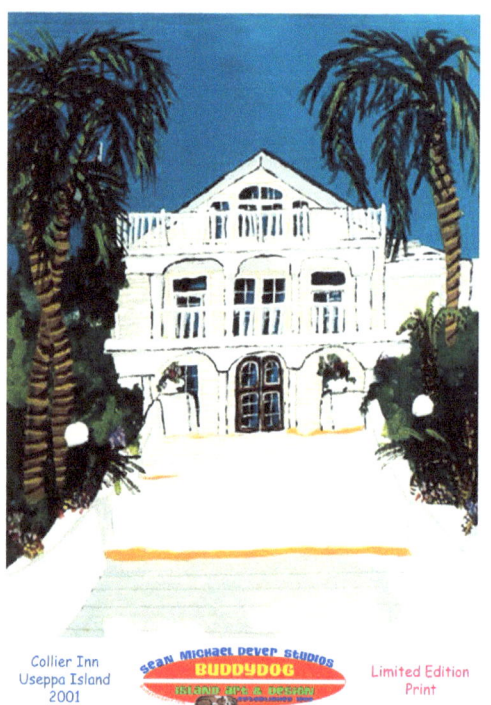

Collier Inn
Useppa Island
2001

#013

Limited Edition
Print

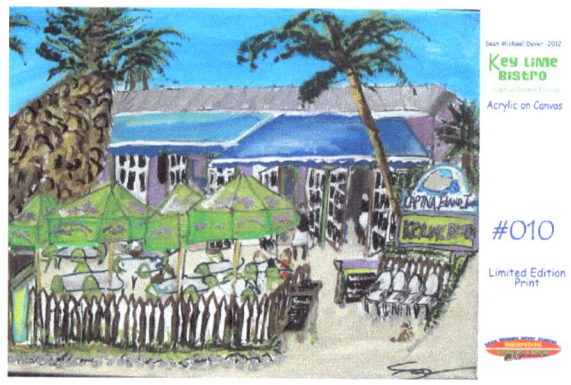

Sean Michael Dever 2012
Key Lime
Bistro
Captiva Island, Florida
Acrylic on Canvas

#010

Limited Edition
Print

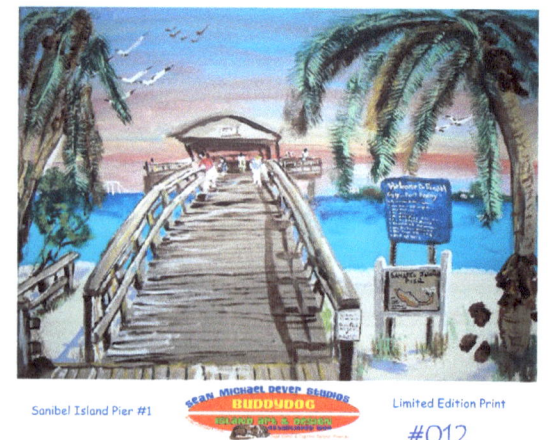

Sanibel Island Pier #1

Limited Edition Print

#012

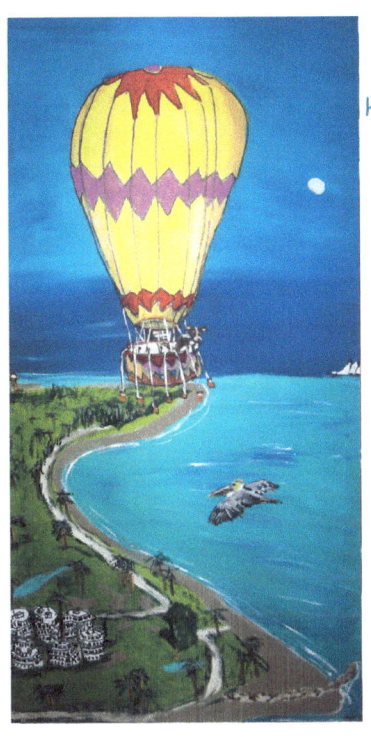

Hot Air Balloon
over
South Seas
Captiva, FL
#008
Acrylic on Canvas
2011

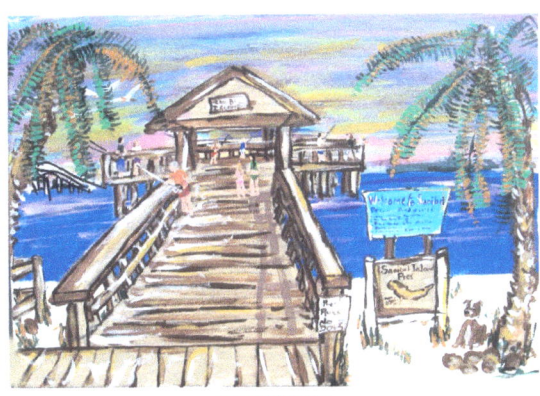

Sanibel Island Pier #2

Limited Edition Print
#022

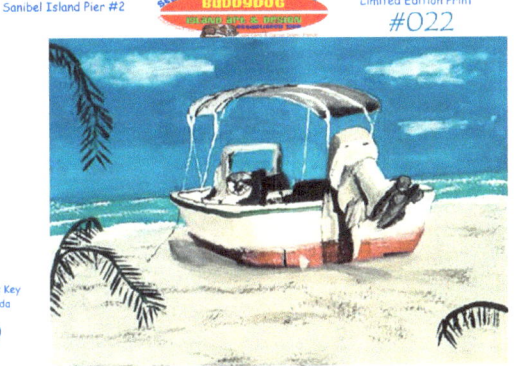

Beached on Lover's Key
Fort Myers, Florida

#029

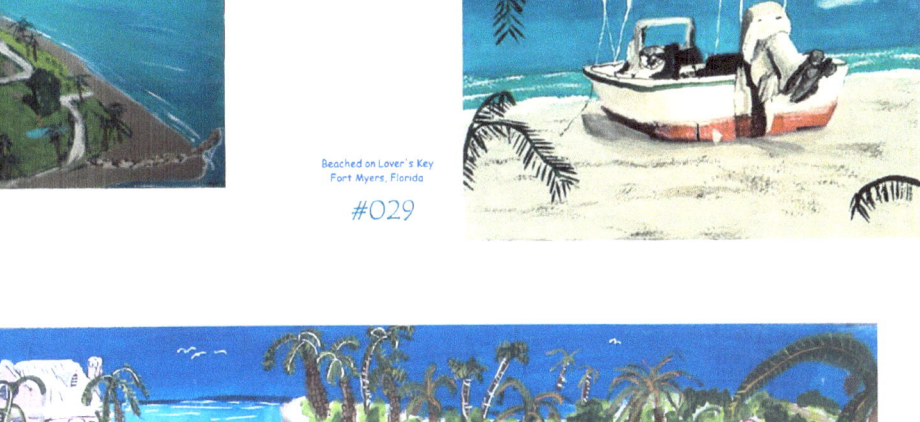

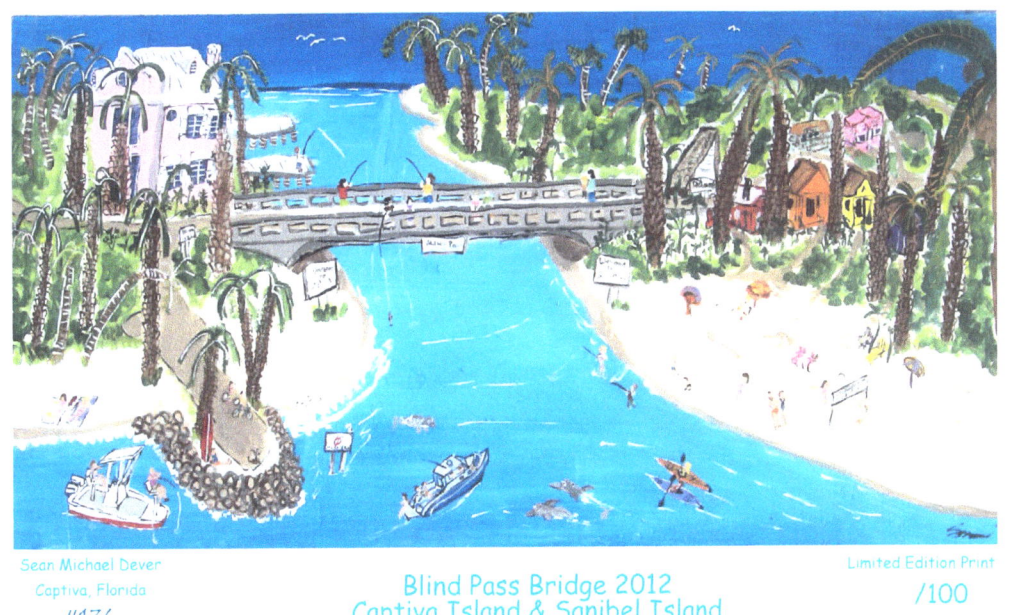

Sean Michael Dever
Captiva, Florida
#136

Blind Pass Bridge 2012
Captiva Island & Sanibel Island
Acrylic on Wood

Limited Edition Print
/100

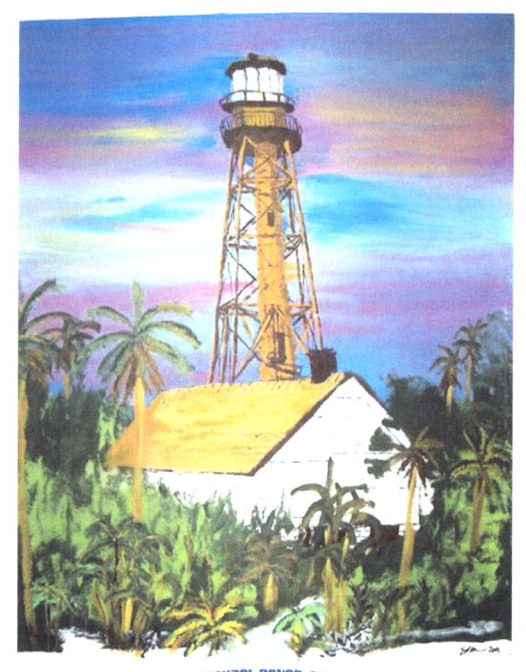

Sanibel Lighthouse
2001

#031

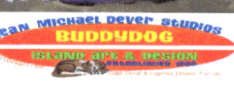

Limited Edition
Print

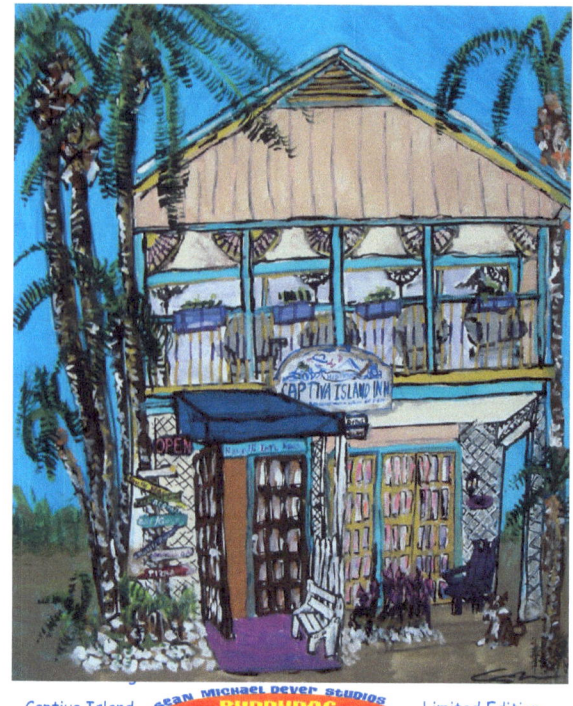

Captiva Island
Inn #1

#020

Limited Edition
Print

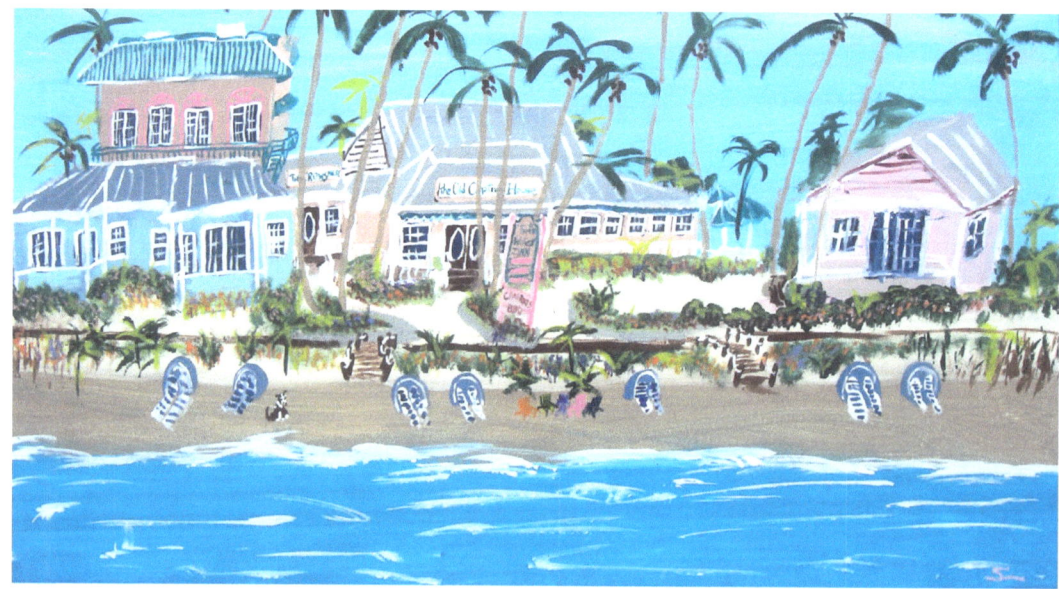

Sean Michael Dever
BuddyDogArt.com
Captiva, FL

#170

'TWEEN WATERS INN, CAPTIVA ISLAND

Limited Edition Print

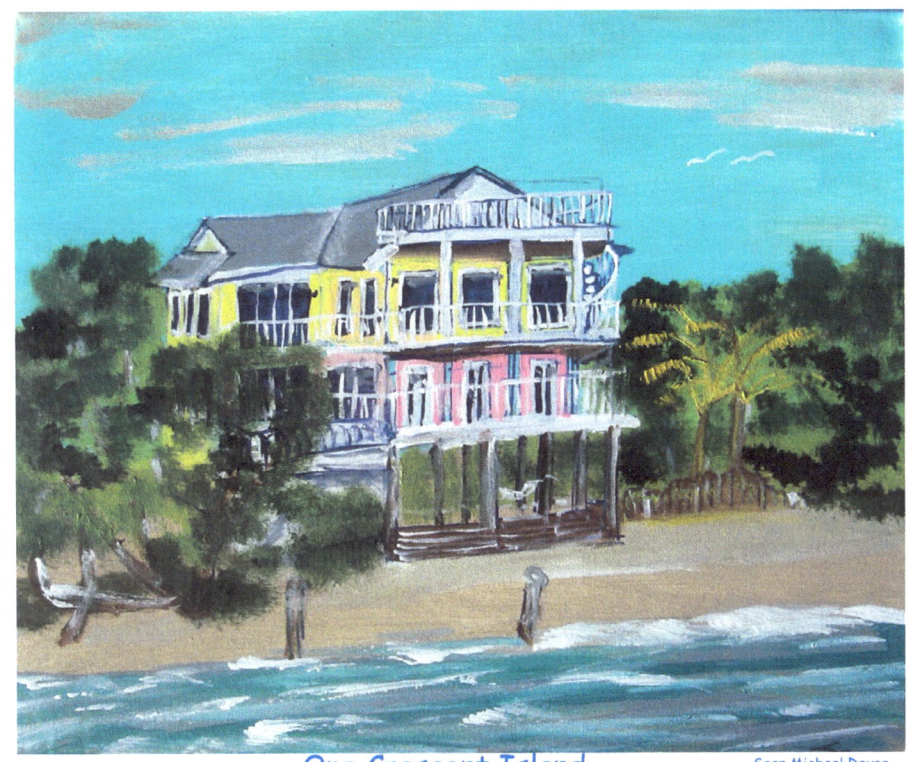

Limited Edition Print
#105A

One Crescent Island

Sean Michael Dever
Acrylic on Canvas

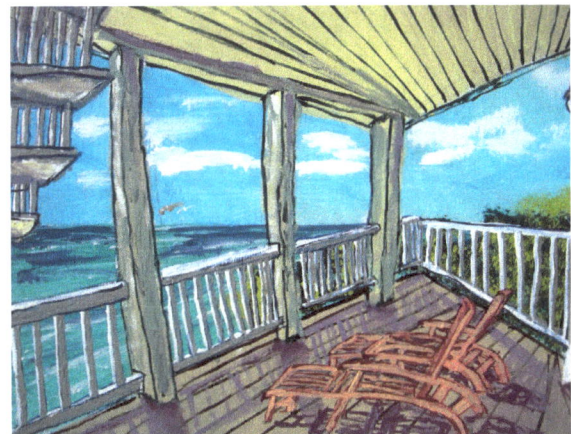

#113 Crescent Island Sundeck

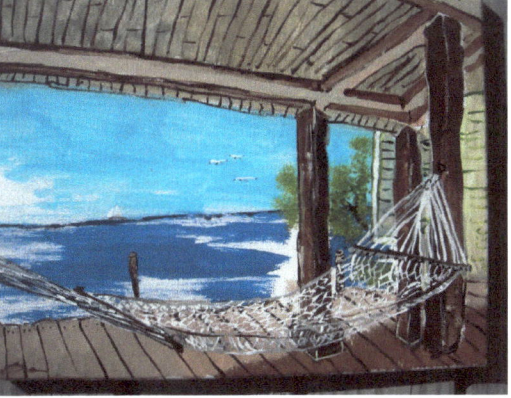

#112 Crescent Island Hammock

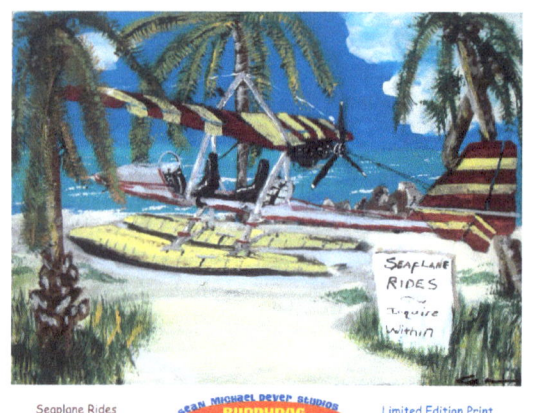

Seaplane Rides
#047

Limited Edition Print

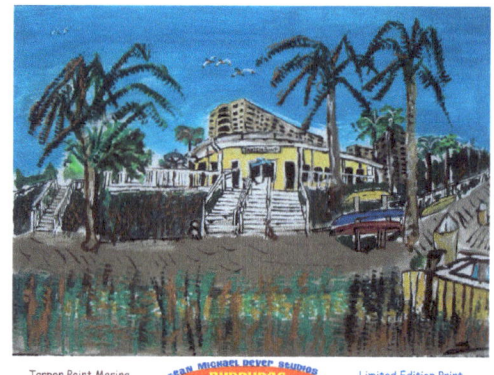

Tarpon Point Marina
Cape Coral, FL

Limited Edition Print
#049

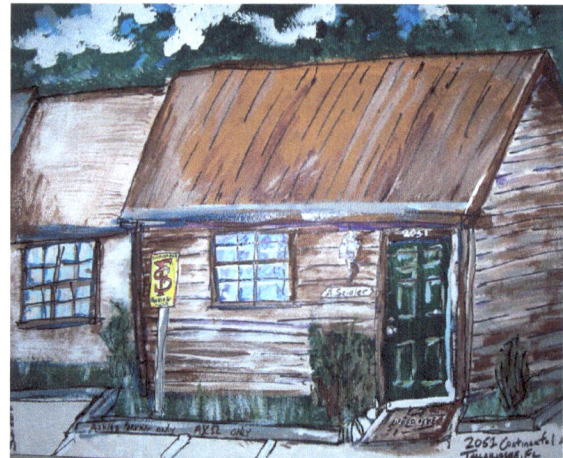

#079 Asley's Tallahassee Apartment

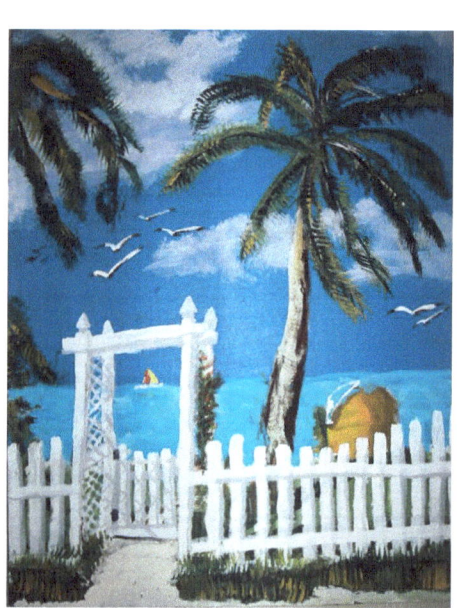

#095 Bokeelia

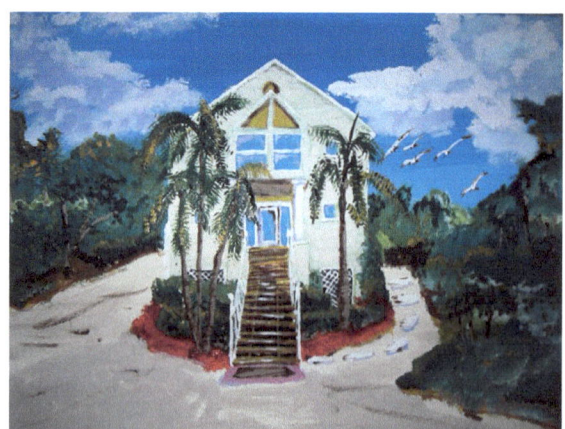

#060 Captiva House

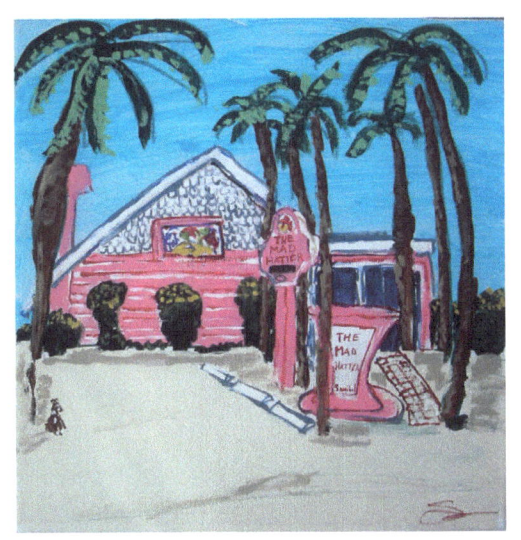

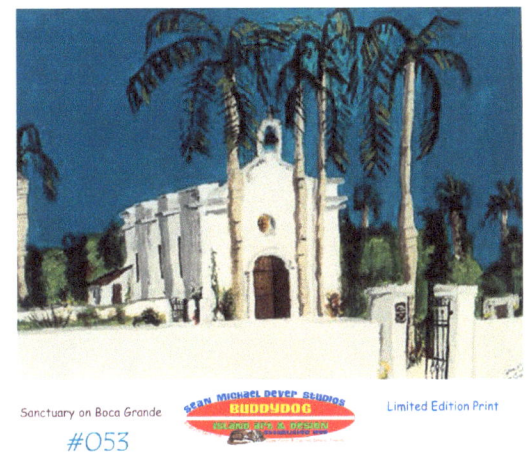

Sanctuary on Boca Grande

#053

Limited Edition Print

#076

The Mad Hatter
Sanibel Island, FL

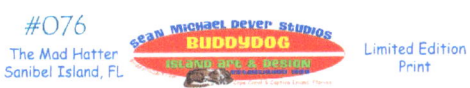

Limited Edition
Print

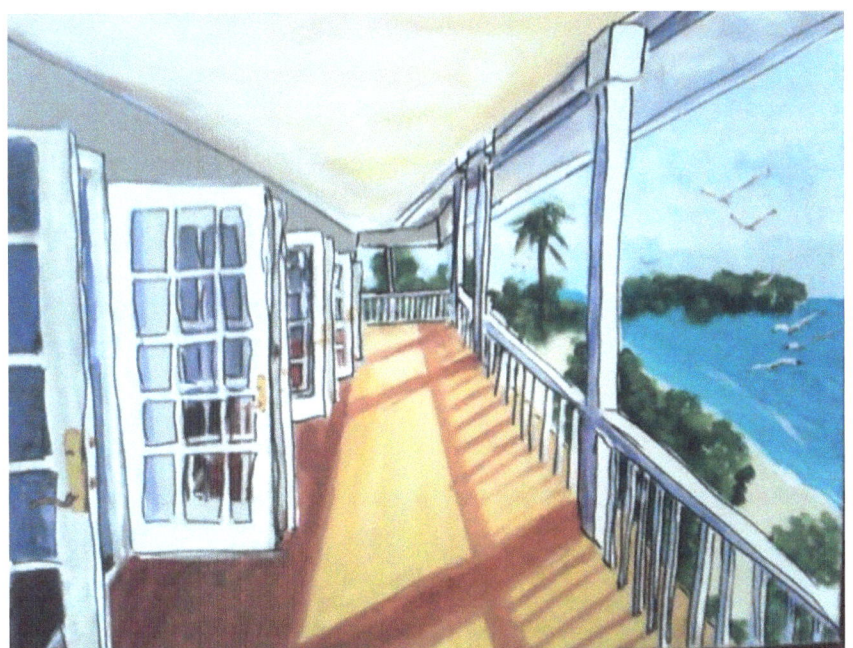

#072 Ussepa Windows

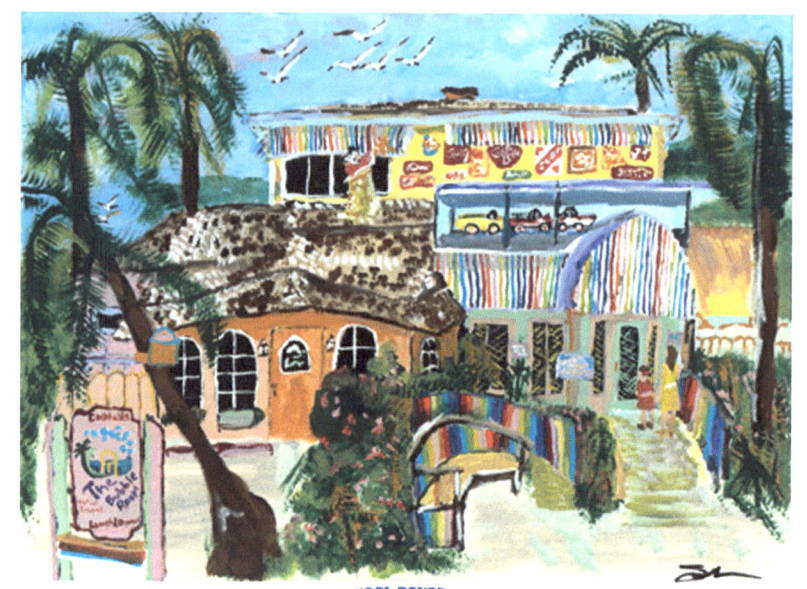

The Bubble Room
Captiva Island

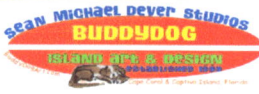

Limited Edition Print

#O96

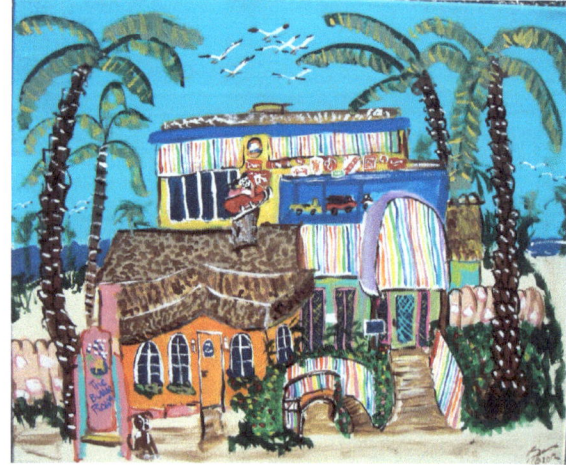

#241 Bubble Room No.2

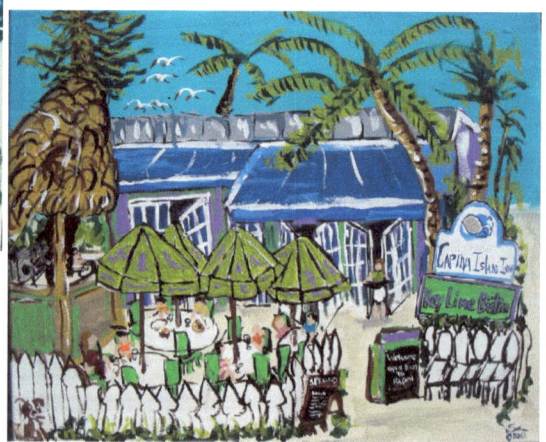

#239 Key Lime Bistro No.3

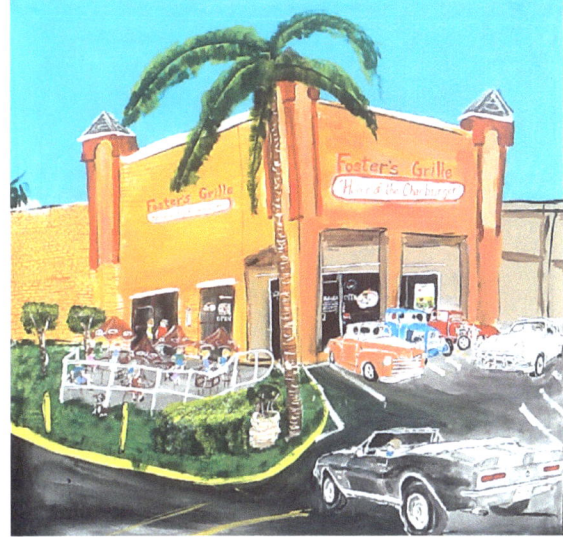

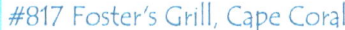
#817 Foster's Grill, Cape Coral

#815 Miami Beach

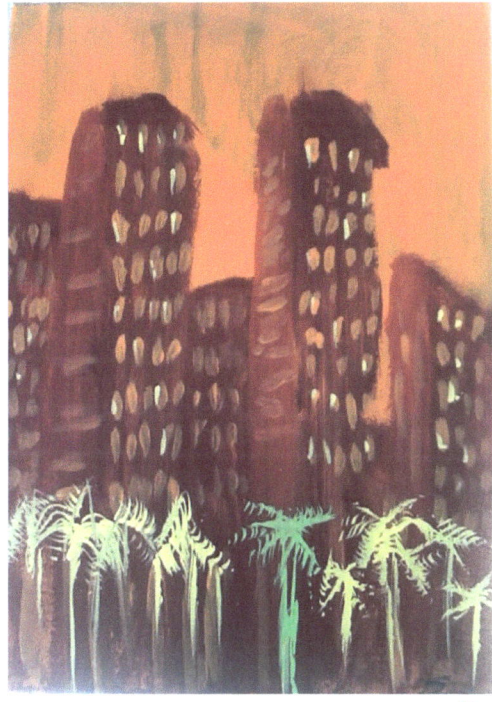

Miami Beach
sean michael dever

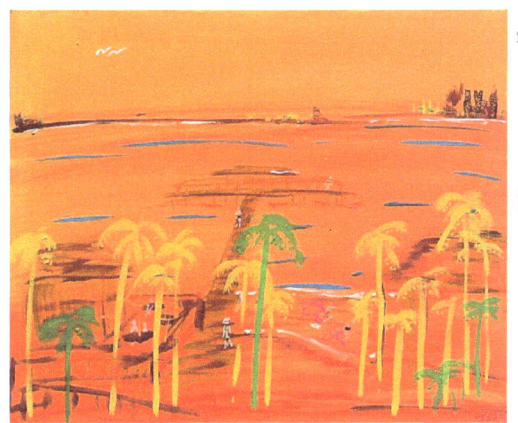

#600 Sloppy Joe's Bar
Key West

Sean Michael Dever
LIMITED EDITION PRINT

#264

cape coral
yacht club & pier
2012
acrylic on canvas

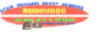

61

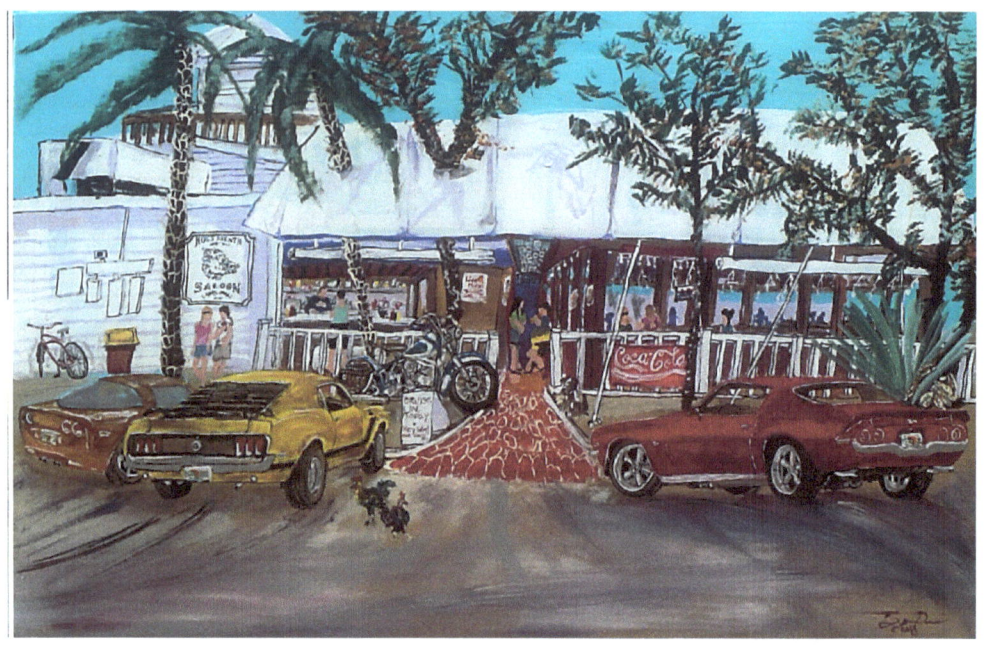

#818 Hog's Breath Saloon, Key West

#816 Fuccillo Kia

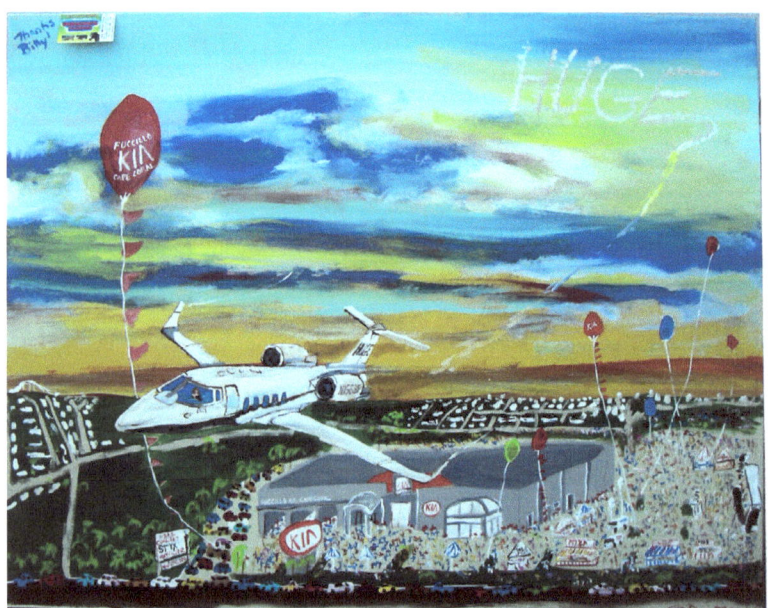

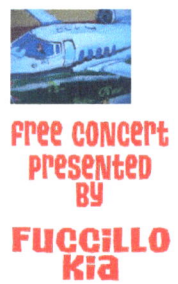

free concert
presented
by

FUCCILLO
KiA

PAINTING BY

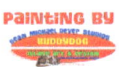

MEMORIAL DAY CONCERT
cape coral, florida   may 31, 2012

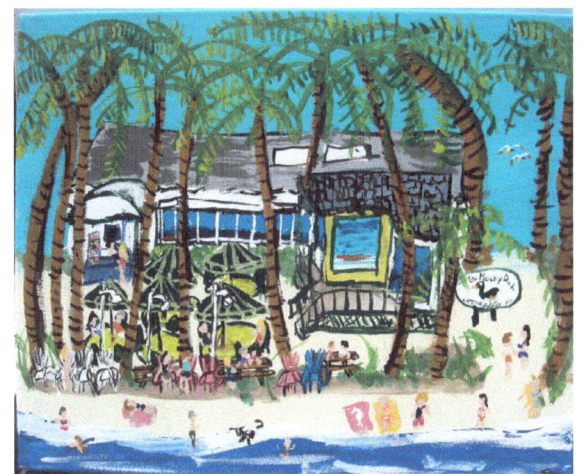

#236 Mucky Duck, No.4

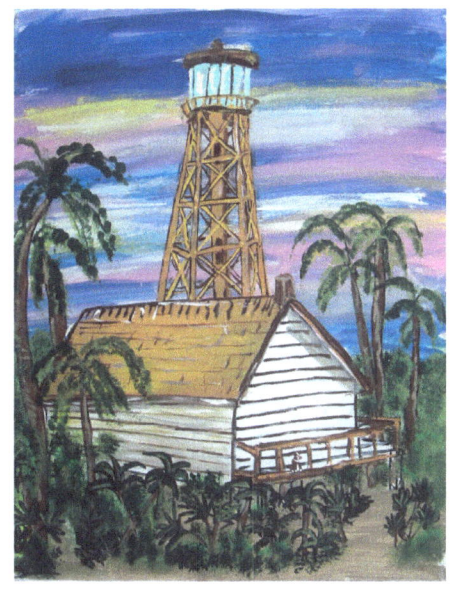

Sanibel Lighthouse 2011
#174

Limited Edition Print

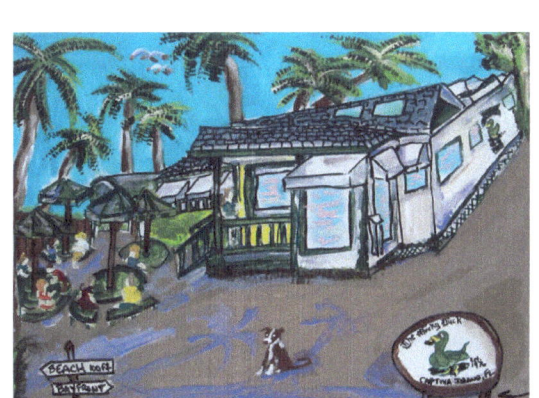

The Mucky Duck Captiva Island

Limited Edition Print

#237 Mucky Duck No.3

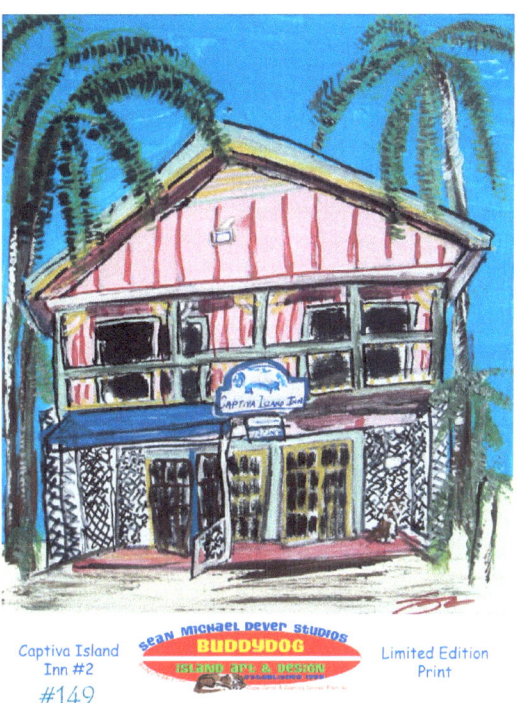

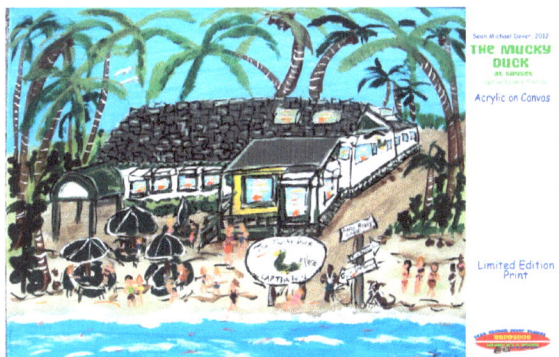

#141 Sunset at the Mucky Duck

Captiva Island Inn #2
#149

Limited Edition Print

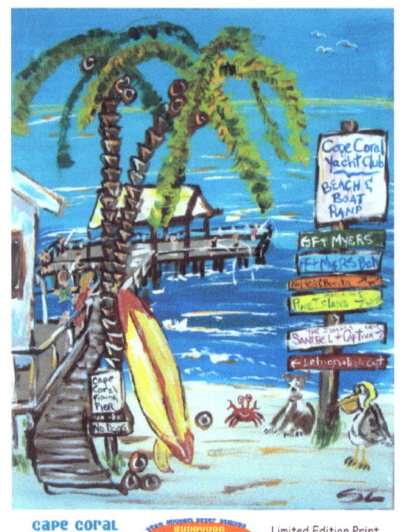

cape coral FISHING PIER
#212

Limited Edition Print

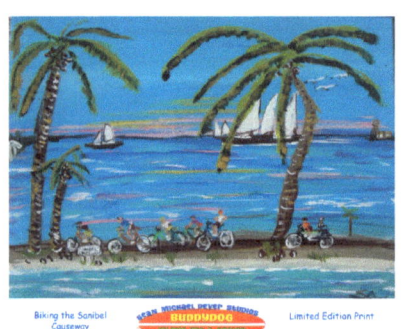

Biking the Sanibel Causeway

#180

Limited Edition Print

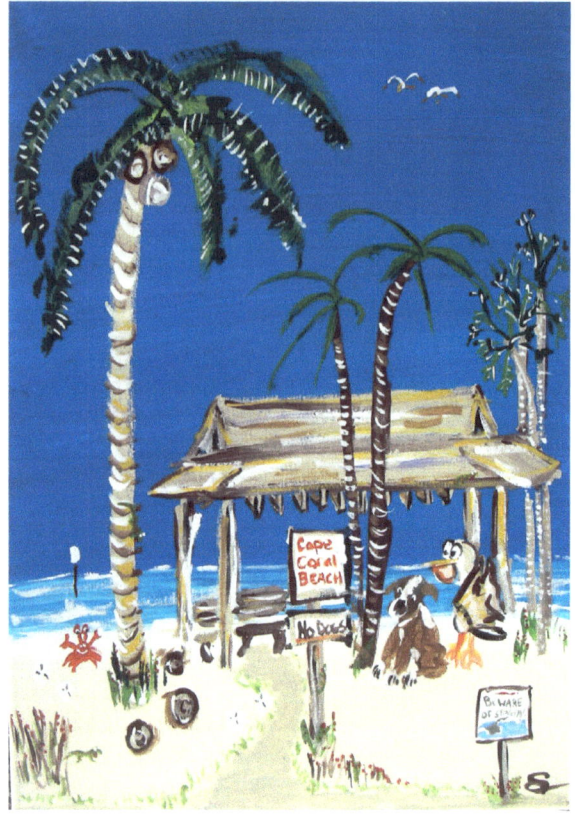

Cape Coral Beach
#222

Limited Edition Print

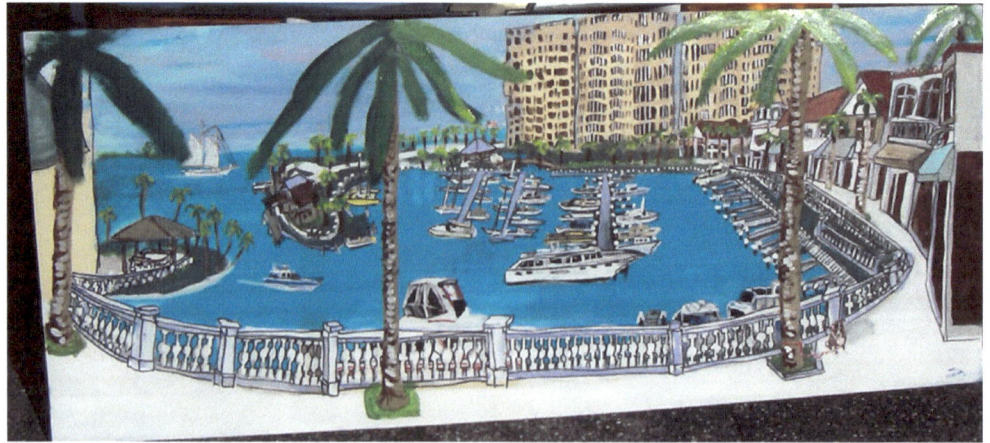

#181 Tarpon Point Marina

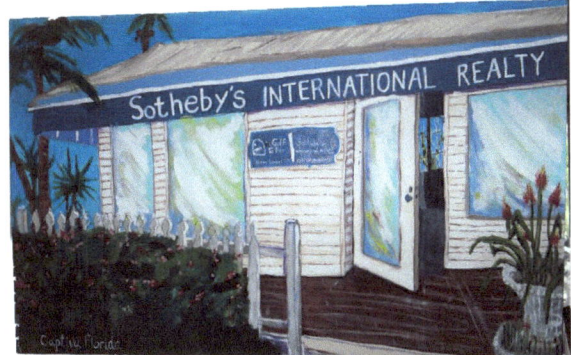

#080 Sotheby's Gulf to Bay Captiva

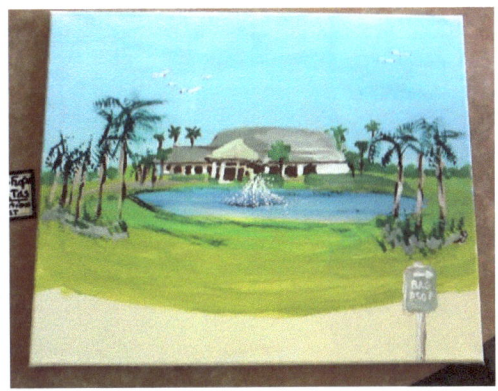

#119 Palmetto Pines

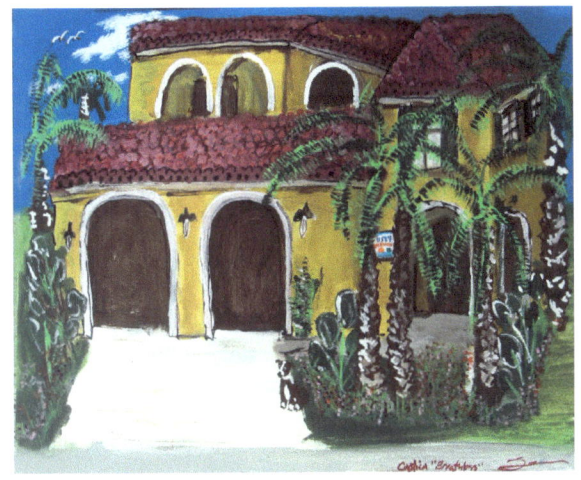

#101 Brethless, Andy Rosse Lane, Captiva

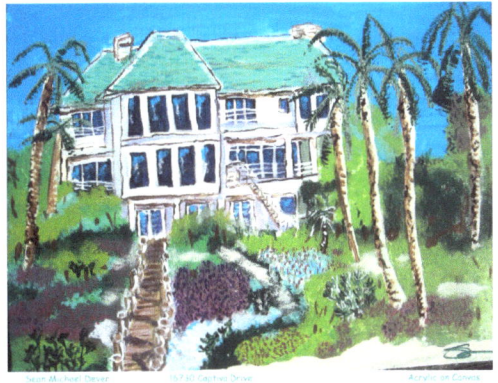

#121 16730 Captiva Drive

#099 Pfiefer Realty Group Xmas Elves, Sanibel

#100 MargaritaVilla, Captiva

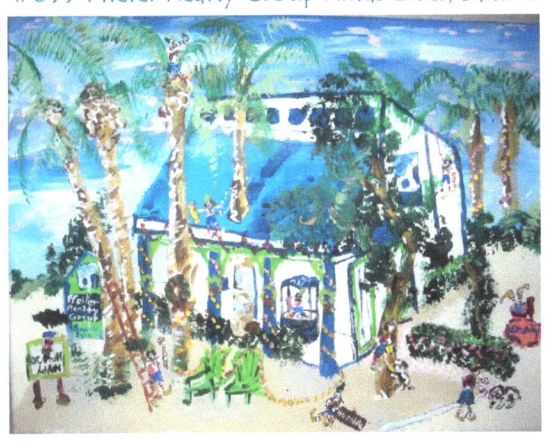

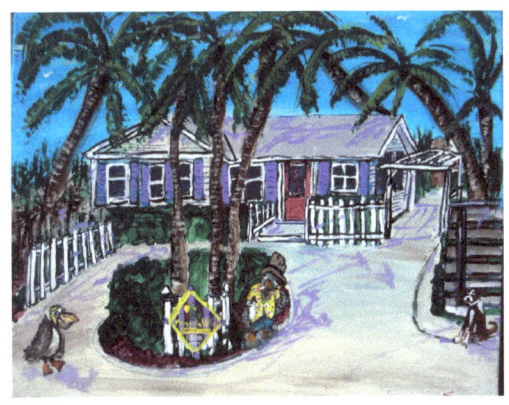

MargaritaVilla, Captiva Island

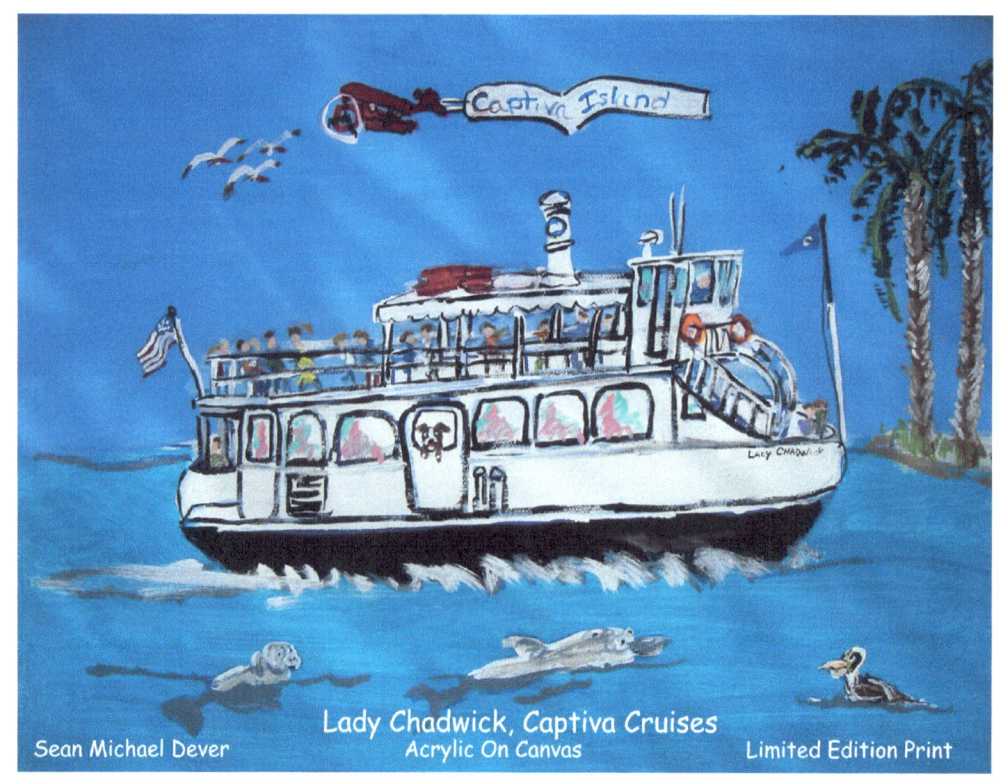

Lady Chadwick, Captiva Cruises
Sean Michael Dever   Acrylic On Canvas   Limited Edition Print

#122 Captiva Cruises

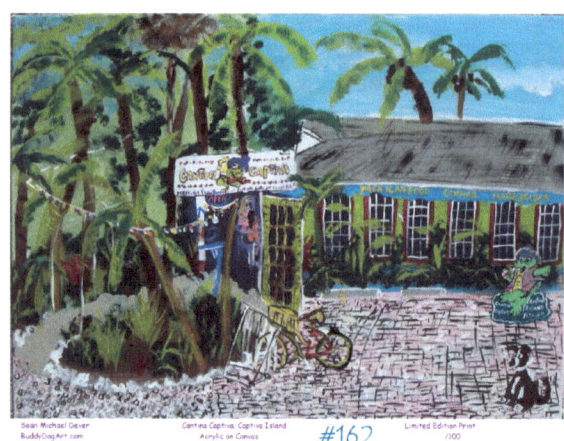

Sean Michael Dever
BuddyDogArt.com   Captiva Captiva, Captiva Island   Limited Edition Print   #162
Acrylic on Canvas   /100

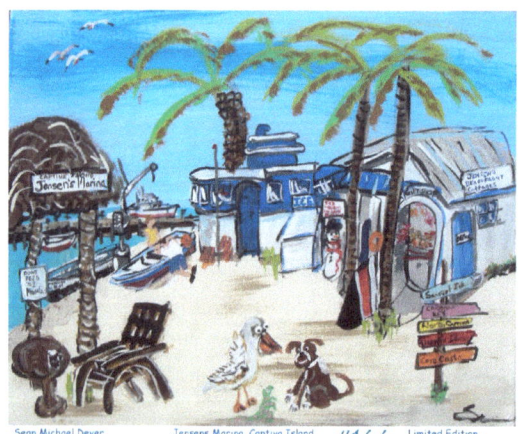

Sean Michael Dever
BuddyDogArt.com   Jensens Marina, Captiva Island   #164   Limited Edition
Acrylic on Canvas   Print

Captiva Island

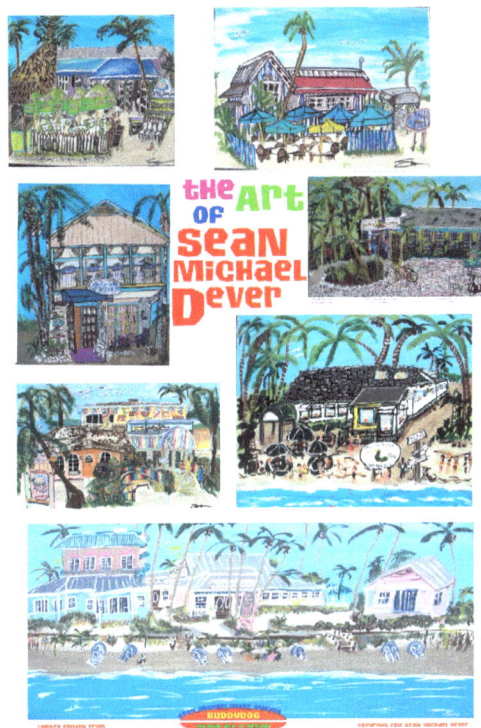

The Art of Sean Michael Dever

#158 Captiva Restaurants

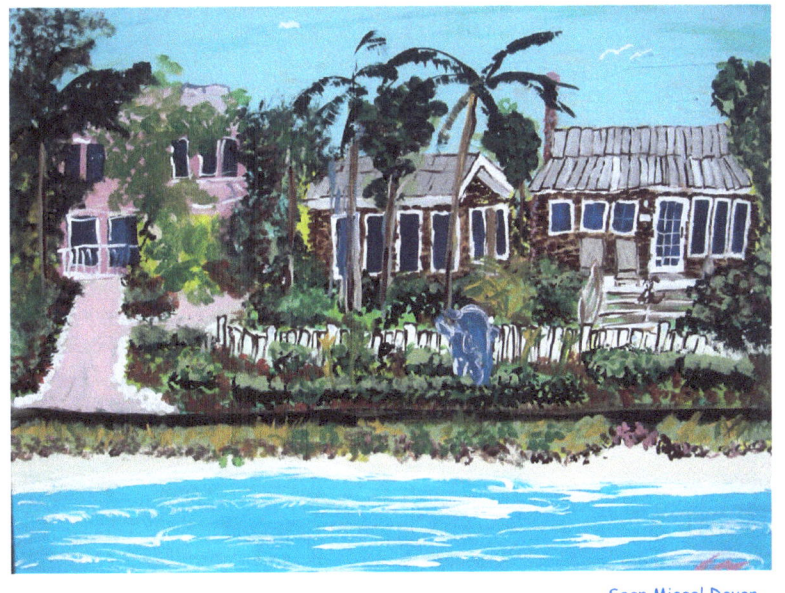

#204 Captiva Gulf Beach Bungalow

Bungalow on the Gulf of Mexico
Captiva Island 2012
Acrylic on Canvas

Sean Micael Dever
Limited Edition Print

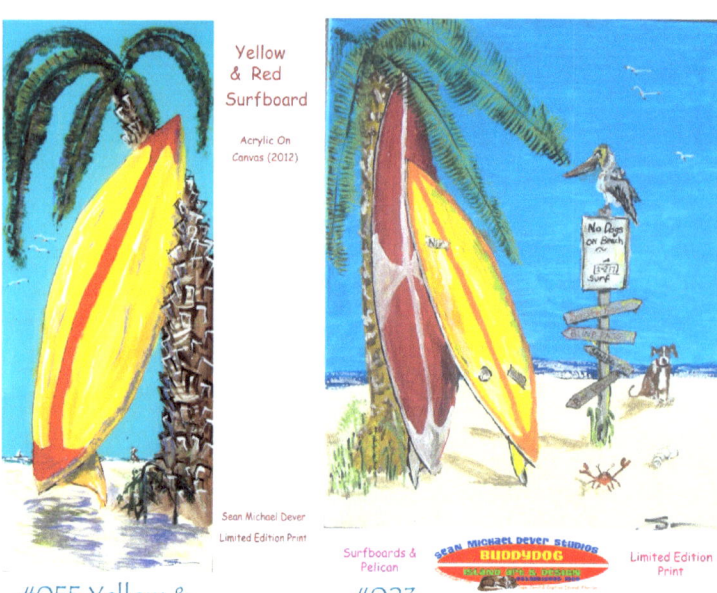

Yellow & Red Surfboard

Acrylic On Canvas (2012)

Sean Michael Dever
Limited Edition Print

Surfboards & Pelican

#023

Limited Edition Print

#055 Yellow & Red Surfboard

#015 Surfboards No.2

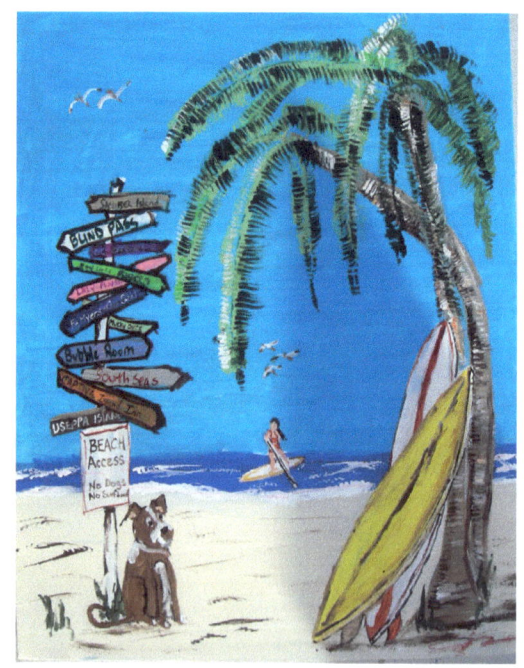

#043 Paddleboarding

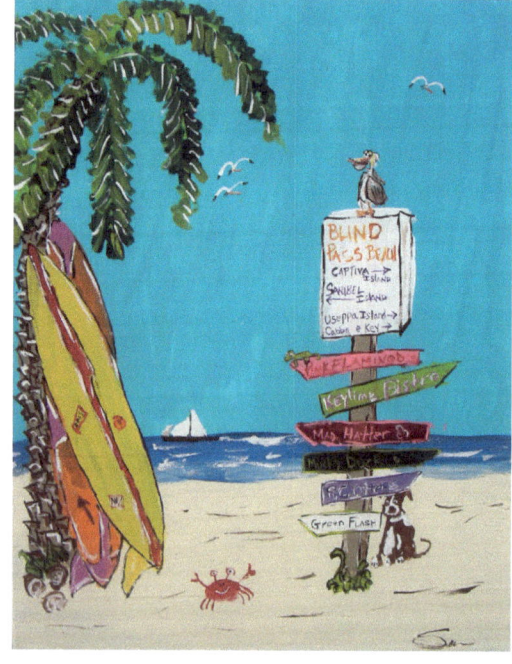

Blind Pass Surfboards & Signpost

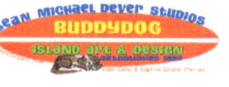

Limited Edition Print

#066

Wood Signs

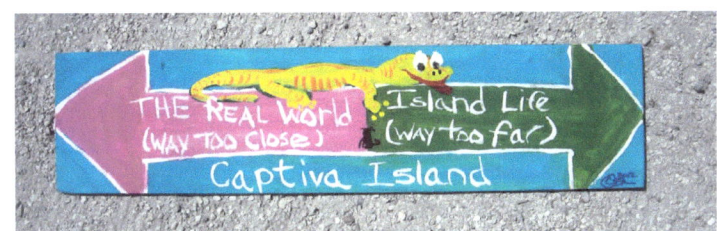

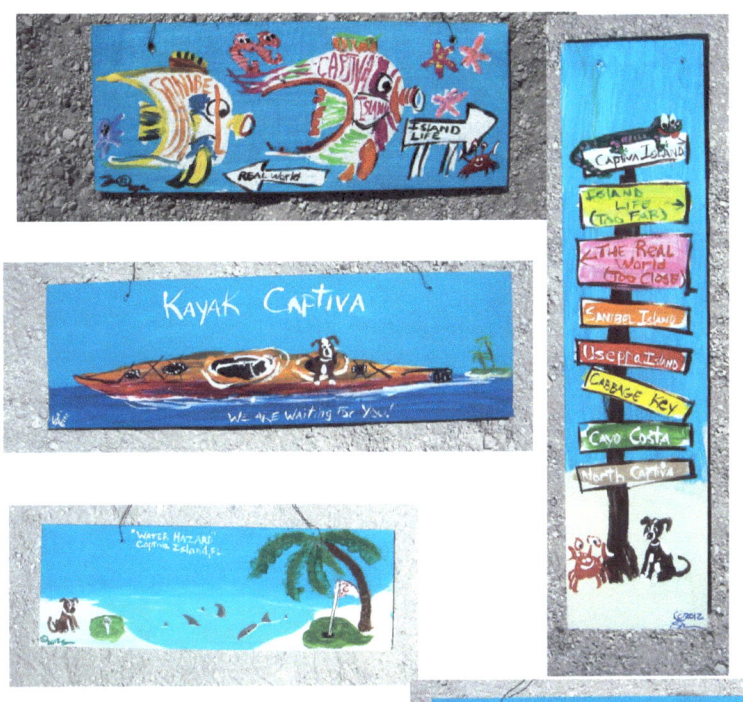

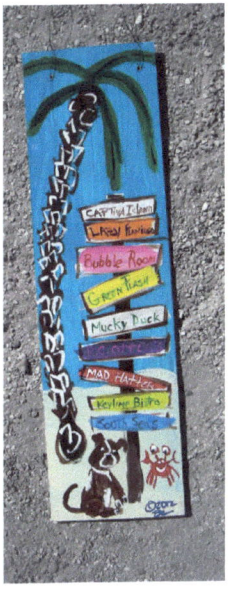

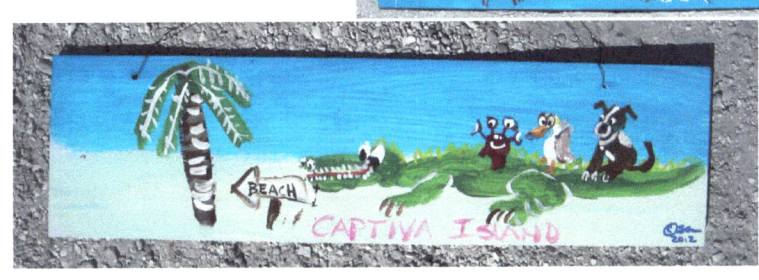

Support these charities by buying a Buddydog Series book or Amazon.com Kindle eBook Download

Military & Shelter Dog Charities
A portion of each book sold goes to help shelter dogs and military dog charities. The following organizations will receive contributions from this fund:

USWarDogs.org
WarriorDogFoundation.org
MissionK9Rescue.org
PawsandStripes.org

Shelter Dogs
Gulf Coast Humane Society
2010 Arcadia Street
Ft. Myers, Florida 33916
239.332.0364

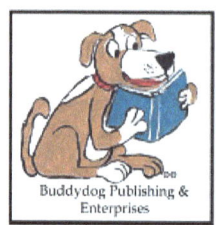

For this book, we will also include CROW on Sanibel island
Clinic for the Rehabilitation Of Wildlife
3883 Sanibel Captiva Road
Sanibel, FL 33957
239.472.3644
Crow Clinic.org

Or reach out and make a donation right now!

www.ingramcontent.com/pod-product-compliance
Lightning Source LLC
Chambersburg PA
CBHW051026180526
45172CB00002B/485

9 7 8 1 0 7 6 2 2 5 2 5 2